Wedding Planner and Organizer

Plan the Wedding saving the Budget, Starting 12 months before with Checklist, Budget Planning, Guests List and Worksheets

Table of Contents

Introduction

The proposal was perfect. The ring is gorgeous. Your engagement is everything you wanted it to be—but when it comes to planning the actual wedding, you don't know where to start. Well, congratulations on taking the first step in the process and thank you for downloading The Wedding Planner and Organizer!

Once the rush of your engagement wears off, you may begin to feel overwhelmed by the thought of planning such a big event. Don't panic! This book provides a step-by-step guide for achieving your perfect day—no matter your budget! Whether you want to have a casual $2,000 reception or an elegant $25,000 affair, this book will help you choose what's right for you.

The following chapters provide a detailed 12-month timeline that walks you through how to choose a wedding date to the moment you say "I do". If you have friends or family who were recently married, you know there are varying opinions on when you should complete certain wedding planning tasks. To help keep you organized throughout the process, this book offers a structured format that will give you plenty of time to accomplish every task listed for that month. Therefore, this book will serve you best if you follow the timeline and cross tasks off the checklist as you go. However, each wedding is unique, so you don't have to follow the advice presented in this book word for word. Instead, tweak the suggestions to your individual wedding and skip those that don't apply.

Throughout the book, you will find tips and tricks that can help save you hundreds, if not, thousands, of dollars on your wedding. The purpose of these is to help you stick as close to your budget as possible without sacrificing the elements you want. You will also find worksheets and checklists to keep you organized; you can fill these out as you go along!

There are plenty of books about wedding planning on the market, so thank you again for choosing this one. Every effort was made to ensure it is full of as much useful information as possible. Please enjoy!

12 Months Before the Wedding

This chapter will cover the three most important steps in planning your dream wedding: choosing a date, creating a budget, and picking a venue. We highly recommend beginning this process as early as twelve months before your wedding— the more time you dedicate to these large tasks, the less stress you'll encounter down the road!

Before you begin, purchase a binder that you can use to organize the most important details of your wedding. Start by adding inspiration from bridal, lifestyle, food, and even gardening magazines! Your binder should be a go-to resource for staying organized as you plan, as well as a hub for important documents.

Choose a Date

The first step in planning any wedding is to choose a date. While this may sound as easy as pointing at a calendar and picking a day, there are many considerations you should keep in mind. Do you want to plan your wedding around a significant event (your first date or first kiss)? How about a particular season (will your ideal venue be impacted by the weather)? Discuss these things as a couple and make sure you're both on the same page.

First, decide on a timeframe together—season and month, for example—and begin narrowing down your options. As a general rule of thumb, do not pick a date that falls on a holiday weekend—and there are many of them! Have a calendar listing all federal, religious, and cultural holidays on hand when choosing a date. If you *want* your wedding to fall on a popular holiday such as New Year's Eve, keep in mind that your venue may be more expensive and not every guest will be able to attend. It's also important not to choose a day of remembrance or a major sporting event. Pencil these dates onto your calendar so you remember to steer clear of them.

Once you confirm that the potential date(s) you choose does not fall on a holiday, day of remembrance, or sporting event, make sure it doesn't interfere with a personally significant date, either. These can include high school/college reunions, family anniversaries, and even other weddings! Mark these on your calendar as well.

Another consideration when choosing a wedding date is where you and your partner plan on spending your honeymoon. Some couples choose to plan their wedding date around their honeymoon, and some choose to plan their honeymoon around their wedding date. Discuss with your partner how flexible your honeymoon location is, and decide from there. For example, if you and your partner are set on honeymooning in the Caribbean, keep in mind that hurricane season generally runs from June to the end of November. Write down a list of possible honeymoon locations and research whether or not there are times of the year you should avoid for each one.

The final consideration in choosing a wedding date is the day of the week you would like to be married on. Saturdays are the most popular wedding days, but this means it is also the most expensive day of the week to be married on. If you have a more limited budget, consider having your wedding on an "off day"—Friday or Sunday would be the cheaper substitute. If you choose to get married mid-week make sure you and your partner are able to take the time off from work.

Do not rush choosing a date; once a date is chosen, wait a week or two before finalizing the decision. Remember, you and your future spouse are going to be celebrating this date for the rest of your lives!

Think your Budget

Perhaps the most daunting task in planning a wedding is creating a budget. Money can be a sensitive subject, but it is important to begin discussing costs very early in the planning process. You may have heard horror stories about the couple who wound up paying thousands on centerpieces, or the photographer who charged double what a couple was willing to pay. So, how do you avoid similar mistakes? Here are the steps you should take before punching numbers into a spreadsheet:

Type of Wedding and Priorities

Whether a simple backyard reception or an extravagant destination getaway, the type of wedding you have is the biggest factor in dictating the cost. While you don't have to decide specifics this early in the process, you should have a general idea of what you want your wedding to be. Use other weddings you attended as inspiration—which ones did you love, and what aspects did you like most? Once you have an idea in mind, you can begin estimating specific costs.

Wedding Type & Style

Ceremony Types

□ Religious

□ Civil

□ Interfaith

□ Not Legal Ceremony

□ Same Sex

Style

□ Grand	□ Formal	□ Refined
□ Romantic	□ Classic	□ Glamour
□ Vintage	□ Relaxed	□ Intimate
□ Festive	□ Fun	□ Offbeat
□ Etnic	□ Beach	□ Destination
□ Vineyard	□ Religious	□ Elegant
□ Modern	□ Casual	□ Rustic
□ Seasonal	□ Religious	□ Simple
□ Retro	□ Traditional	□ DIY
□ Garden	□ Backyard	

Place

☐ Where you live

☐ Where your parents live

☐ Where your flance's family lives

☐ Far away (destination wedding)

☐ Other _____

Size

☐ Very Intimate / Restricted (50 persons)

☐ Intimate (100 persons)

☐ Average (100-300)

☐ Large (over 300)

☐ Other _____

☐ Number of Guests _____

Season

☐ Spring

☐ Summer

☐ Winter

☐ Autumn

Date: _____

Month : _____

Ceremony Hour

□ Sunrise

□ Midday

□ Evening

□ Sunset

□ Late Night

Time

_____

Color palette

□ Bright and bold

□ Rich jewel tones

□ Earth tones

□ All white

□ Soft pastels

□ Citrus Colors

□ Black with an accent color

□ Metallics / Neutrals

□ Seasonal colors

□ Specific colors _____

Parties (beyond the reception)

☐ Engagement party
☐ After party
☐ Bridesmaid luncheon
☐ Welcome party
☐ Post wedding brunch

Reception priorities (rank from 1 to 10)

_____ Time of year/day of week

_____ Officiant ceremony location

_____ Guest List

_____ Food & drink

_____ Music (band or Dj)

_____ Reception setting

_____ Wedding dress

_____ Flowers and décor

_____ Photo and video

_____ Other _____

Favorite Venue

☐ Farm   ☐ Beach   ☐ Park

☐ Garden   ☐ Ranch   ☐ Resort

☐ Restaurant   ☐ Castle   ☐ Villa

☐ Golf Club   ☐ Yacht Club   ☐ Country Club

☐ Residence   ☐ Vineyard   ☐ Tennis Club

☐ Horses Club   ☐ Stadium   ☐ Lakeside

☐ Other _____

Important Opinions to take into account

☐ You as a couple

☐ Your parents

☐ His / Her parents

☐ Other _____

Use in this space to dream your perfect wedding, fill additional information not mentioned in the previous pages or other important things to consider.

_____

_____

_____

_____

_____

Couple

Bride

☐ Wedding Dress

☐ Shoes

☐ Make Up

☐ Accessories & Jewelry

☐ Veil or Headpiece

☐ Wedding Ring

☐ _____

☐ _____

Groom

☐ Suite or Tuxedo

☐ Shoes

☐ Watch

☐ Cuff Links

☐ Lapel Pin

☐ Socks

☐ Wedding Ring

☐ _____

Wedding Party

Bridesmaids

□ Bridesmaid Dresses

□ Jewelry

□ Shoes

□ Gifts

□ _____

Groomsmen

□ Suits or Tuxedos

□ Shoes

□ Ties

□ Socks

□ Gifts

Flower Girl

□ Flower Girl Dress

□ Flower Girl Jewelry

□ Flower Girl Basket

□ Flower Girl Gift

Ring Bearer

□ Ring Bearer Outfit

□ Ring Pillow or Box

□ Ring Bearer Gift

□ _____

Guestbook Attendant

□ Attire

□ Gifts

Ushers

□ Attire

□ Gifts

Ceremony

Traditions

☐ Standard Vows

☐ Self Written Vows

☐ Special Readings

Miscellaneous

☐ Marriage License

☐ Officiant

☐ Guest Book

☐ Programs

☐ _____

☐ _____

☐ _____

Music

☐ Playlist

☐ Special Songs

☐ Live Musicians

Florals

☐ Altar

☐ Bridal Bouquet

☐ Bridesmaid

☐ Bouquets

☐ Boutonnieres

☐ Family Boutonnieres

☐ Family Corsages

☐ Miscellaneous Florals

Reception

Beverages

- □ Coktail Hour
- □ Beer and Wine
- □ Champagne
- □ Open Bar
- □ Not Alcoholic Beverages
- □ Toast

Food

- □ Appetizers
- □ Buffet Meal
- □ Full Service Meal
- □ Late Night Snack
- □ Desserts
- □ Wedding Cake
- □ Groom's Cake

Favors

- □ DIY
- □ Purchased
- □ Plants
- □ Edible
- □ Charitable Donations
- □ Personalized

Rental Equipment

- □ Lighting
- □ Dance Floor
- □ Rental Decor
- □ Tent
- □ Lounge Furniture
- □ _____

Entertainment

- □ Dance Party
- □ Karaoke
- □ Photo Boot
- □ Games
- □ _____
- □ _____
- □ _____

Tradition

- □ Receiving Line
- □ Dances with Parents
- □ Toasts or Speeches
- □ Wedding Party Intro
- □ Garter Toss
- □ Couple Intro

□ _____

□ _____

Table and Seating

□ Dinner Tables

□ Coktail Tables

□ Chairs

□ Centerpieces

□ Place Cards

□ Seating Charts

□ Flatware

□ Desposable Cutlery

□ Monogrammed Napkins

□ Linens

□ Table Runners

Transportation

□ Limo

□ Bus

□ Getaway Car

□ _____

□ _____

□ _____

□ First Dance

□ Couple Intro

Music

□ DJ

□ Live Band

□ Play List

□ _____

□ _____

□ _____

□ _____

□ _____

□ _____

□ _____

□ _____

Paper Goods

□ Save the Dates Cards

□ Invitations

□ Thank You Cards

□ Calligraphy

□ Signage

□ Printed Menu

Discuss With Your Partner Where the Money is Coming From

First, determine the total amount of money you and your partner can comfortably put towards the wedding. Once this amount is determined, you should discuss whether or not you need/want others to contribute as well. Outside contributions most often come from family, but it's important to keep in mind that not every family member will be willing or able to help financially. Approach the topic delicately, and never demand that they contribute a specific amount. If you are appropriate and tactful, most families will be more than happy to help out. You can also ask that they cover a specific expense, rather than donating a random amount.

Once you have determined if you will be receiving outside contributions, open a savings account specifically for your wedding so that you can keep track of how much money you have to cover expenses.

Tip:
While not part of the wedding, your honeymoon will be another major expenditure that you need to plan for around this time.

Who pays for what ?

Legend to compile the table (signs to put in the columns)

- Y (yes) indicating who pays for the related item
- N (no) indicating the spouses give up
- Blank indicating the decision has to be taken

Item	Bride	Bride's Family	Groom	Groom's Family
Grooms wedding ring				
Grooms wedding gift				
Bredesmaids gifts				

Personal Stationery				
Brides Engagement & Wedding ring				
Brides Wedding Gift				
Gifts for best man and groomsmen				
Marriage Licence				
Clergy or judge Fee				
Brides Boquet				
Coursages				
Boutineers				
Transportation				
Invitations				
Services of Bridal Consult				
Wedding Gift for the Couple				
Brides Gown, Veil and accessories				
Their own attire				
Bridesmaids Luncheon				
Rental of Wedding Site				
Music for Church and Reception				
Flowers for Church				
Bridesmaids Boquets				
Transportation for Bridal Party				
Reception				
Fee				
Catering				

Wedding Cake				
Music				
Decorations				
Flowers				
Gratuities				
Photography				
Videography				
Engagement Photos				
Lodging for out of Town Guests				
Their own Wedding Attire				
Their own Travel and Lodging				
Wedding Gift for the Couple				
The Rehersal, Dinner or Luncheon				
Purchase of Apperal and all Accessories				
Transportation to and from the Wedding City				
Gift from all the Bridesmaids to the Bride				
Bridal Shower or Luncheon				
Wedding Attire				
Transportation to and from the Wedding City				
Gift from all the Groomsmen to the Groom				
Bachelor Party				

Choose the Number of Guests

The number of guests you invite can make or break a budget. Both partners should create a fantasy guest list, then be realistic. From that list, choose the people you are obligated to invite—usually immediate and extended family members, and best friends. Create a separate list for colleagues, co-workers, or acquaintances who you would like to have at your wedding but don't necessarily need to invite. These people can join the first list once you decide whether or not you can afford it. For now, use the list of people you are obligated to invite as your estimate. You may also add 10% more guests to this list since usually, 10-20% of the people you invite will decline. Having an estimated number of guests will be crucial moving forward – not only will your budget be affected by it, but the venue you choose as well.

Bride's Potential Guests List

Family Members

_____

_____

_____

_____

_____

_____

_____

_____

_____

_____

_____

_____

_____

_____

_____

_____

_____

_____ : _____

_____

_____

Others Guests

_____

_____

_____

_____

_____

_____

_____

_____

Groom's Potential Guest List

Family Members

Others Guests

Number of potential Guests estimation

Bride's Number of Guests: _____

Groom's Number of Guests: _____

Couple Number of Guests = Bride's Number of Guests + Groom's Number of Guests =
_____

Tot Number of Guests = Couple Number of Guests + 10% = _____

Bride's Final Guest List

Family Members

Others Guests

Gromm's Final Guest List

Family Members

_____

_____

_____

_____

_____

_____

_____

_____

_____

_____

_____

_____

_____

Others Guests

Number of Final Guests

Bride's Number of Guests: _____

Groom's Number of Guests: _____

Couple Number of Guests = Bride's Number of Guests + Groom's Number of Guests
            = _____

Tot Number of Guests = Couple Number of Guests + 10% = _____

Create your Budget

Once these basic steps are covered you can begin to create a more detailed budget. By now you should have determined the maximum amount you're willing and able to spend.

Below is an example of a detailed budget based on the current average people spend on their weddings: $25,000.

However, your budget might be quite smaller. The example is followed by a blank worksheet for you to customize your very own budget.

Tip:

Determine the hard maximum for your wedding budget and plan to spend 15-20% lower than that. For example, if your maximum is $10,000, try to keep costs around $8,000-8,500. This will provide a buffer in your budget for unexpected costs or last-minute additions.

Example of budget creation

The following table is an example useful to estimate your wedding costs starting from your available budget.

The following table should be used to assign the % to each main items costs.

For example:

Macro Item cost	Average Cost %
Venue, Food, and Beverages	42-50%
Ceremony Specifics	2–3%
Photography/Videography	18–20%
Décor	8–18%
Stationary/Paper Goods	3–7%
Attire	8–10%
Entertainment	6–10%
Planner/Coordinator	5–15%
Miscellaneous	2–8%
Emergency Fund	4–5%

The reader of course can modify these percentages as he likes at own budget estimation section (see chapter Create your real budget estimation)

How to use the budget Planning Worksheet

This is an example about how to use the budget estimation table using the % in the previous table just only for the first macro item cost **(Venue, Food, and Beverages)**

<table>
<tr><td colspan="7">(SAMPLE)
Maximum Projected Budget: $25,000</td></tr>
<tr>
<td></td>
<td>Average cost %</td>
<td>Budget Estimae</td>
<td>Total Actual Cost</td>
<td>Deposit Amount Paid</td>
<td>Remain Balance</td>
<td>Final Pay Due Date</td>
</tr>
<tr>
<td>Venue, Food, and Beverages</td>
<td>42% 50%</td>
<td>$10,50 0$12,5</td>
<td>$9,300</td>
<td>$3,250</td>
<td>$6,050</td>
<td>15th Sept 2018</td>
</tr>
<tr>
<td>Venue (ceremony)</td>
<td>15%</td>
<td>$3,750</td>
<td>$3,000</td>
<td>$1,000</td>
<td>$2,000</td>
<td></td>
</tr>
<tr>
<td>Venue (reception)</td>
<td>15%</td>
<td>$3,750</td>
<td>$3,000</td>
<td>$1,000</td>
<td>$2,000</td>
<td></td>
</tr>
<tr>
<td>Catering (including food, service, etc)</td>
<td>7%</td>
<td>$1,750</td>
<td>$1,500</td>
<td>$750</td>
<td>$750</td>
<td></td>
</tr>
<tr>
<td>Bartending/ Beverage and cake</td>
<td>8%</td>
<td>$2,000</td>
<td>$1,800</td>
<td>$,500</td>
<td>$1,300</td>
<td></td>
</tr>
</table>

Create your budget estimation

Macro Item cost	Average Cost %
Venue, Food, and Beverages	
Ceremony Specifics	
Photography/Videography	
Décor	
Stationary/Paper Goods	
Attire	
Entertainment	
Planner/Coordinator	
Miscellaneous	
Emergency Fund	

(CREATE YOUR OWN)

Maximum Projected Budget: ....$

	Average Cost %	Budget Estimate	Total Actual Cost	Deposit Amount Paid	Remain Balance	Final Payment Due Date
Venue, Food, and Beverages						
Venue (ceremony)						
Venue (reception)						
Catering (including food, service, dinnerware, glassware, utensils, etc.)						

	Average Cost %	Budget Estimate	Total Actual Cost	Deposit Amount Paid	Remain Balance	Final Payment Due Date
Photography Videography						
Photographer						
Videographer						
Décor						
Flowers (for Yourself and Venue decorations)						
Other decorations (centerpieces, guestbook, wedding arch, etc.)						

+

	Average Cost %	Budget Estimate	Total Actual Cost	Deposit Amount Paid	Remain Balance	Final Payment Due Date
Lighting						
Rental furniture (tables, chairs, linens, etc.)						
Stationary/ Paper Goods						
Save the Date cards						
Invitations (including RSVP cards)						
Other cards (menu, program, escort cards, etc.)						

	Average Cost %	Budget Estimate	Total Actual Cost	Deposit Amount Paid	Remain Balance	Final Payment Due Date
Postage stamps						
Attire						
Attire for both the bride and groom						
Hair and makeup						
Entertainment						
DJ/Band/etc.						

	Average Cost %	Budget Estimate	Total Actual Cost	Deposit Amount Paid	Remain Balance	Final Payment Due Date
Planner/ Coordinator						
Miscellaneous						
Transportation, photobooth, gifts, favors, extra fees, tips, wedding night hotel, etc.						
Emergency Fund						
Always try to have 4–5% set aside for last minute or unexpected expenses						

Vendor Payment Plan

Ceremony	Vendor	Dep. $	Due Date	TOT $	Due Date
Ceremony Site					
Musicians					
Decorators					
Florist					
Wedding Planner					
Officiant					
Photo -Grapher					
Video -Grapher					
Tuxedo					
Gown					
Manicurist					
Hair Stylist					
Make-Up Artist					
Hotel					
Transportation					
Reception					
Reception Site					
Caterer					
Baker					
Bartender					
DJ / Musiciants					

Decorator					
Florist					
Honeymoon					
Flight					
Hotel					
Other					

Contacts

Wedding contacts

Wedding Planner

Name:
_____

Address:
_____

Phone / Mobile Phone
_____

Email:
_____

Website:
_____

Note
_____

Jewelery

Name:
_____

Address:
_____

Phone / Mobile Phone
_____

Email:
_____

Website:
_____

Note
_____

Ceremony Venue

Name:
_____

Address:
_____

Phone / Mobile Phone
_____

Email:

Website:

Note

Officiant

Name:

Address:

Phone / Mobile Phone

Email:

Website:

Note

Caterer

Name:

Address:

Phone / Mobile Phone

Email:

Website:

Note

Musicians

Name:

_____

Address:

_____

Phone / Mobile Phone

_____

Email:

_____

Website:

_____

Note

_____

Dressmaker

Name:

_____

Address:

_____

Phone / Mobile Phone

_____

Email:

_____

Website:

_____

Note

_____

Photographer

Name:
_____

Address:
_____

Phone / Mobile Phone
_____

Email:
_____

Website:
_____

Note
_____

Videographer

Name:
_____

Address:
_____

Phone / Mobile Phone
_____

Email:
_____

Website:
_____

Note
_____

Florist

Name:

Address:

Phone / Mobile Phone

Email:

Website:

Note

DJ

Name:

Address:

Phone / Mobile Phone

Email:

Website:

Note

Rental Company

Name:

Address:

Phone / Mobile Phone

Email:

Website:

Note

Baker

Name:

_____

Address:

_____

Phone / Mobile Phone

_____

Email:

_____

Website:

_____

Note

_____

Rehearsal Dinner Venue Manager

Name:

_____

Address:

_____

Phone / Mobile Phone

_____

Email:

_____

Website:

_____

Note

_____

Transportation Contact

Name:

_____

Address:

_____

Phone / Mobile Phone

_____

Email:

_____

Website:

_____

Note

_____

Hair Stylist

Name:

_____

Address:

_____

Phone / Mobile Phone

_____

Email:

_____

Website:

_____

Note

_____

Makeup

Name:

_____

Address:

_____

Phone / Mobile Phone

_____

Email:

_____

Website:

_____

Note

_____

Wedding Night Hotel

Name:
_____

Address:
_____

Phone / Mobile Phone
_____

Email:
_____

Website:
_____

Note
_____

Hotel for Out of Towners

Name:
_____

Address:
_____

Phone / Mobile Phone
_____

Email:
_____

Website:
_____

Note
_____

Honeymoon contacts (Travel Agent)

Name:

_____

Address:

_____

Phone / Mobile Phone

_____

Email:

_____

Website:

_____

Note

_____

Flight Company

Name:

_____

Address:

_____

Phone / Mobile Phone

_____

Email:

_____

Website:

_____

Note

_____

Accomodation

Name:

_____

Address:

_____

Phone / Mobile Phone

_____

Email:

_____

Website:

_____

Note

_____

Very important: *Ckeck your passports validity and expiration date*

Pick a Venue

There's no doubt about it: your venue will set the tone of your wedding day. Next to deciding a date, choosing a venue can be the most difficult aspect of planning a wedding, which is why it's important to begin the process early.

As stated in the previous section, your venue will be largely determined by your budget and the number of guests you intend to invite. Rather than feeling constrained by this, use your budget and guest list to eliminate obvious no-go's.

Next, begin looking at venues that align with your vision.

Dreaming of a rustic, outdoorsy wedding? See if there are barns or parks in your area that host weddings. How about cozy and traditional? Look at churches and schedule a time to meet with the priest to discuss your options. Small budget? Consider having the wedding in you or your partner's backyard—it would make what is usually the largest expenditure completely free!

Next, it is important to consider your guests. If you and your partner's families live far from each other, you will have to determine if you want the venue to be closer to one family or in the middle. The venue should have hotel accommodations relatively close by for those who are traveling a great distance.

Once you have a general idea of the type of venue you're after, begin researching your options. Use the checklist below to keep track of important information regarding each one:

Tracking Information about Venue at Site Visit Time

Venue name:

_____

Website:

_____

Location:

_____

Availability:

_____

Maximum guest capacity:

_____

All inclusive (yes/no)?:

_____

Facility extras:

_____

Nearest hotel:

_____

Parking and transportation:

_____

Total estimated cost:

_____

After narrowing down your search to three or four venues using the criteria above, it's time to arrange site visits to see which is the perfect fit.

Site visits are crucial, so make sure you and your partner set time aside for them. For instance, the venue you're eyeing may look completely different from what is shown on the website. Visiting the venue in advance will help you clear up any uncertainties. Therefore, it's important to go prepared with a list of questions.

Some questions you may want to ask are:

Questions to do at Site Visit Time

1. **Does the venue include a rehearsal dinner/ceremony?** If yes, find out when it takes place and how far in advance you need to book it.

2. **How long is the rental for?** Setting up usually takes about two hours and cleanup takes around one. Make sure the remaining time is enough for the ceremony and reception. If not, discuss the prices for extra hours.

3. **What's the cancellation policy?** Ask the latest date you can cancel by and still get a partial or full refund.

4. **Is there a backup space for an outdoor venue?** This is an important question in case of bad weather.

5. **Is there an in-house caterer or preferred caterers?** If using your own, ask where the caterer can set up.

6. **Can the venue accommodate a live band or DJ?** If yes, also discuss whether or not there are volume restrictions or a time when the band/DJ has to stop playing.

7. **What is the alcohol policy (if there is one)?** Some venues do not allow dark liquor in case of spills, for example.

8. **Does the host recommend any nearby hotels?** You may know of the closest hotels, but venue hosts can offer you more information on which are the best options.

9. **What kind of lighting does the venue have?** While you may be visiting during the day, wedding ceremonies often occur at night. Make sure you know what the lighting situation is, and whether or not you will need extension cords for different accessories.

10. **What are the hidden fees associated with the venue?** You don't want to be blindsided at the last second with hidden fees. Don't be shy about requesting an exact price breakdown.

11. **Were the other couples married there, satisfied of the services ?**
Ask for references from couples who were married there to see if their experiences align with your expectations.

Check list

There are 12 months until your wedding!

Have you...

Actions 12 months	Done Y/N
Chosen a date	
Created a budget	
Picked a Venue	

If not, consider completing these important steps before moving on to the next chapter.

NOTES

_____

_____

_____

_____

_____

_____

_____

_____

_____

_____

11 Months Before the Wedding

With the major details of your wedding decided, it is time to begin delving deeper into specifics. This chapter details the steps you should take at least 11 months before your big day.

Finalize and Book Your Venue

Before signing, make sure you read the contract *very* carefully to make sure all of the information is correct.

Actions to do before finalize the venue booking:

1) **Try the food and beverage** *making a lunch choosing some of the recipes of the wedding menu.*

2) **Decide the detailed menu and beverage**

3) **Negotiate a lower price**:
   There may be extra amenities you don't plan on using, and you can ask to have these subtracted from the total cost. While negotiating has its limits, this can be a way for you to bring the total cost down and save extra money later on.

4) **Before signing the contract**
   make sure you read the contract *very* carefully to make sure all of the information is correct.

Detailed contract for Venue Reservation

A detailed contract for Venue Reservation: should contain the following:

- Your name and contact information, as well as contact information for the venue

- Reception date and time

- Description of the venue space you will be using (wall/floor colors, lighting, etc.) and all amenities included

- Floor plan, including the number of tables and number of seats at each

- Proof of liquor license

- Detailed menu and beverage

- Setup and cleanup times
- Total cost
- Amount due as an initial deposit
- Remaining balance and payment dates
- Cancellation and refund policy

Once you are satisfied with the accuracy of the contract, sign it and breathe a sigh of relief. Your venue is now finalized!

Hire a Wedding Photographer

Your next major task is to hire a wedding photographer. This is important to tackle early in the planning process, especially if you and your partner plan on having engagement photos taken as well.

If you don't know much about photography and are unsure of where to start, considering following these steps:

Questions to choose the Photographer:

First, know what style you and your partner like.

1) **Do you like darker, more emotional photographs?**
   If yes, consider choosing a photographer who specializes in black and white.

_____

_____

_____

_____

_____

_____

2) How about sunny, naturally lit photographs?
   If yes, find a photographer who regularly shoots outdoor weddings.

_____

_____

_____

_____

_____

3) Do We like the other books of our photographer ?

_____

_____

_____

_____

_____

4) How can we take more ideas ?
   This is also a good time to ask for recommendations from friends and family. Take a
   look at their wedding albums and keep note of what aspects you like most.

_____

_____

5) Is the Venue Space and Environment compatible with the type of photography we want ?

Now that your venue is finalized, you should consider your venue space when researching photographers. If you are choosing a photographer based on the type of photography they excel at, make sure it's compatible with your venue.

Lighting is a key factor here! While a good photographer should be able to take excellent photos in any setting, some venues are more conducive to a certain style. Keep this in mind as you begin looking at various portfolios.

6) Do we like the photographer's style ?

_____

_____

_____

_____

_____

7) What is included in the photography package ?

_____

_____

_____

_____

_____

8) How long it will take to receive the photos ?

_____

_____

_____

_____

_____

9) Have we full rights to the images ?

_____

_____

_____

_____

_____

10)   Has the photographer experience shooting at our type of venue ?

_____

_____

_____

_____

_____

Which are the feedback of other couples ?

_____

_____

_____

_____

_____

_____

Note: Most importantly, don't skimp out when choosing a photographer. Though the amateur photography student may seem enticing because their rates are so low, it's best to go with a reputable photographer who charges a professional rate. Unlike other aspects of your wedding, the photographs are going to stick around for a long time. You should aim for the best quality possible!

Keep in mind:

1) Agree with the photographer an accounts for approximately 10% of your budget.

2) Don't become invested in a particular photographer only to find out you can't afford their fees, but have a realistic price in mind and keep your search as close to that as possible. Photographers keep their prices competitive; if you can't afford one that you really like, chances are another couple can.

3) The average cost is around $2,000, but it varies depending on the photographer's experience, the number of hours they shoot, and what is included in their package.

> **_Tip:_**
>
> If you want to save money on a photographer, consider hiring them for fewer hours. Have them skip the pre-wedding activities and take your own fun photographs with a disposable or Polaroid camera instead.

Engagement Shots	
Outfits	
Formal Attire:	
Casual Attire:	
Groom Outfit 1:	
Bride Outfit 1:	
Groom Outfit 2:	
Bride Outfit 2:	
Groom Outfit 3:	
Bride Outfit 3:	
Locations	
Beach	
Park	
Field	
Shared Home	
Urban Setting	
Cafe	
Twirling	
Shots	
Holding Hands	
Kissing	
Similar At Each Other	
Formal Pose	
Running	
Piggy Back	
The Ring	

Photography Shots	
Prep Shots	
Dress Hanging / draped	
Bride's Ring	
Mother zipping / buttoning Dress	
Bride doing / fixing air	
Bride in the mirror	
Bride pinning flower's on parents	
Parents handing bride boquet	
Bride's Shoes beneath her dress	
Groom fixing air	
Parents pinning flowers on groom	
Groom in the mirror	
Bride / Groom entering / exiting limos	
Venue	
Venue's exterior (empty)	
Venue's exterior (guests arriving)	
Venue's interior (empty)	
Venue's interior (guests arriving)	
Altair / canopy	
Rings on pillow	
Band / DJ	
Ceremony	
Groom entering church	
Parents being seated	
Grandparents being seated	
Groom waiting at altar	
Bride waiting in foyer	
Maid of honor entering	

Bridesmaids / Groomsmen entering	
Flower girl entering	
Ring bearer entering	
Bride and father entering	
Groom's reaction	
Guests reactions	
Front / side / back of bride	
Father giving away bride	
Vows	
Exchanging rings (close-up)	
Kiss	
Signing Certificate	
Walking down the aisle	
Receiving line	
Bride / Groom getting in limo	
Bridge / Groom in limo	
Reception	
Venue Exterior	
Venue Interior	
Tables with Favors	
Wedding Cake	
Gift Table	
Guest Book	
Band / DJ	
Bride / Groom entering	
Guests Getting Food / Eating	
Toasts	
Cutting the Cake	
Feeding each Other	
Bouquet / garter toss	
First Dance	
Bride / Father dance	
Groom / Mother dance	

Take out Wedding Insurance

Securing wedding insurance is an important yet underrated step in the planning process. As the age-old saying goes, "Hope for the best, but prepare for the worst." Wedding insurance can cover everything from an unforeseeable storm that closes your venue to a damaged gown.

The most basic policy, which may cover attire, rings, photos, and gifts, usually costs around $150-$500.

Additionally, your venue might already have liability insurance. Double-check this before you pay for overlapping costs.

Every policy is different, so if you choose to take out insurance, be sure to understand what is covered and what is not by talking to an agent. For example, most policies typically don't cover engagement rings, other forms of jewelry, or the worst-case scenario—cold feet. Some wedding-related items may also require you to take out a supplemental policy.

In the end, wedding insurance not only offers you financial protection but also peace of mind. It doesn't account for a large portion of your overall budget, and it's totally worth it.

Choose Your Wedding Party

Now is the time to start thinking about who will serve as the best man, maid of honor, groomsmen, and bridesmaids. Not only do the best man and maid of honor stand by the altar as you exchange vows, they traditionally help out with a number of important tasks! Therefore, while a best man and a maid of honor aren't *required*, they do tend to be a huge help during the planning process. Best man duties typically include organizing the bachelor party, assisting during suit shopping, and day-of tasks (such as organizing ushers and delivering a toast). Maid of honor duties are usually more involved and include hosting the bridal shower and bachelorette party, organizing bridesmaids, helping with décor, and keeping track of gifts.

If you or your partner choose not to have a best man/maid of honor, make sure you aren't taking on too much responsibility while planning the rest of the wedding. Delegate tasks that would normally fall to these people to the rest of your wedding party. On the flip side, if you find yourself in a situation where you are trying to choose between your sister and best friend for the maid of honor, don't be afraid to have both! This will help avoid hurt feelings.

Tip:

In most weddings, the couple traditionally pays for the best man's suit. If you are expecting a financial contribution from the best man, it is important to be honest and let them know up front.

There is no limit on the number of groomsmen and bridesmaids you're required to have, but, in general, most couples choose to have an equal number of both (for example, photos tend to look better with five groomsmen and five bridesmaids than two groomsmen and seven bridesmaids—but again, this isn't a requirement). Most weddings generally have between three-five of both, but don't feel pressured to have a "perfect" number.

As the groom, make it a point to call the guys you plan on asking to be your groomsmen. Better yet, meet up in person to ask as this is way more formal than sending a text or an e-mail. As the bride, you may want to ask your family/friends if they would like to be a bridesmaid in a creative way (think of it as your way of "proposing" to them!). This may consist of sending a small box of gifts, getting matching t-shirts/outfits, or hosting a group dinner date. While not required, it's a fun way of showing your appreciation.

The important thing is to include those closest to you in your wedding party, and those who will continue to be a big part of your life after the wedding is over.

Go Dress Shopping

Dress shopping is one of the most exciting parts of wedding planning. No matter what type of bride you are, you'll want to find a dress that fits your personality, style, *and* budget. Finding the perfect dress takes time and energy, so it's important to prepare for the process.

Do your research beforehand. Dresses come in all styles, so going into an appointment with an idea of what you want in mind will streamline the process. The six most common dress styles are A-line, ball gown, empire, trumpet, sheath, and mermaid. There are several different necklines to choose from as well, including V-neck, strapless, scoop, halter, and sweetheart. Look at different combinations of styles and keep tabs on what you like best.

It's important to re-establish your dress budget at this time. In Chapter 1, we said that wedding attire should account for about 8-10% of your total budget. However, this includes accessories, alterations, hair/makeup, and the groom's suit. Alterations alone can cost upwards of $250-$500. To save yourself the heartache, don't try on any dresses that are out of your price range! If your dress budget is on the lower side, there are a number of ways you can save:

1. **Shop during sale season.** Many retailers host sales during the winter and summer months to make room for new merchandise.

2. **Rent or buy used one.** Some brides choose not to purchase a wedding dress they'll wear only once, opting to rent instead. Sites such as <u>BorrowingMagnolia.com</u> will rent dresses up to 85% off their retail price! There's also the option of buying gently used. The site <u>OnceWed.com</u> sells used dresses from brides who wore them once.

3. **Buy the floor sample.** If it's in good condition, ask the boutique or salon if you can buy the sample you tried on instead of buying a new version. Some brides have reported getting up to 50% off the dress's retail price!

4. **Choose a gown with less fabric.** In general, the more fabric a dress has, the more expensive it will be. Consider choosing a simpler or more casual dress if you have a smaller budget.

When you decide on where you'd like to shop, call and make an appointment. A typical consultation usually takes about an hour and a half, so don't schedule too many in one day.

Before attending the appointments, you should choose who you'd like to bring. While it seems tempting to invite all the women in your family as well as all your bridesmaids, having a large entourage with numerous opinions can be stressful. Aim to keep your helpers to a minimum—your mother, sister(s), and best friend are more than enough!

On the day of your appointment, make sure you wear the proper undergarments, including nude underwear and a strapless bra at the minimum. You should also consider bringing a pair of Spanx if you want to smooth out your hip and stomach areas. Wear limited makeup; you do not want to risk staining a dress that you're merely trying on. (A small amount of moisturizer, blush, and mascara will do.) Try to mimic the hairstyle you intend on having, as this will give you a better impression of how you'll look in the dress and what accessories you may want.

When trying on dresses, remember to keep an open mind and listen to the advice of your consultant. Wedding dresses are different than your typical gown, and you might not realize you like a certain style until you try it on. Once you've said yes to a dress, don't look back! It's time to relax and look forward to dazzling everyone on your wedding day.

Compile a Guest List

By now, you should have a ballpark estimate of the number of guests you intend on inviting to your wedding based on the list you created in Chapter 1.

Compiling a detailed guest list is not only important for sending invitations, but for keeping track of RSVPs, gift information, and Thank You cards.

RSVP List

Guest Name	Date Invit Mailed	Resp Y/N	# of Guests

Send Save the Date Cards

The final thing you should decide on the initial stages of wedding planning is whether or not to send Save the Date cards. They are optional, but you should consider sending one if:

- You are having a destination wedding
- The majority of your guests will be traveling a great distance to your wedding
- Your wedding is during a busy time of the year (i.e., summer)
- Your wedding falls on a three-day weekend

If any of the above apply, you should plan to send Save the Date cards not later than eight months in advance. Twelve months may sound early, but with schedules filling up earlier and earlier, the more advanced the notice, the better. (This is especially important for destination weddings since your guests will need ample time to plan for traveling abroad.) Even if you are having a local wedding, you may still choose to send Save the Date cards. It's a fun way of getting the word out to your family and friends!

Check list

There are 11 months until your wedding!

Have you...

Actions 11 months	Done Y/N
Finalized your venue	
Hired a photographer	
Taken out wedding insurance	
Chosen your wedding party	
Gone dress shopping	
Compiled a guest list	
Sent save the Date cards	

If not, consider completing these important steps before moving on to the next chapter.

NOTES

_____

_____

_____

_____

_____

_____

10 Months Before the Wedding

Now that you're well into wedding mode, it's time to start planning for the ceremony and reception. Completing the tasks outlined in this chapter will help your wedding begin to take shape —yes, this is really happening!

Decide Your Theme and Colors

Deciding the wedding theme and colors is fundamental in creating a cohesive aesthetic. By now, you should have a good idea of what your theme will be, and it is usually tied to the venue. If you're getting married in a barn, chances are you'll go with "country chic" or a similar variation. If your wedding takes place in a hotel, your theme will probably lean towards "traditional and elegant."

Once your theme is nailed down, you'll have to choose a color scheme. Since many aspects of the wedding depend on the colors, from flower arrangements to the bridesmaids' dresses, it's important to pick them soon after you've chosen a date and finalized the venue.

Begin by choosing a base color. The base color is the color that will occur the most in decorations and attire. When deciding on this color, consider the season of your wedding. If you're getting married when the foliage starts to change, you may want to choose a deeper color such as emerald, navy blue, or plum. These colors naturally go with cooler seasons. If you're getting married in the spring, you may want to go with pastels. For summer weddings, bright and sunny colors are perfect.

Once you have a base color, you should decide on two or three "accent" colors. The accents can be neutral hues that complement the base color or hues that contrast the base color and add a bold look. Keep your venue space in mind when deciding accents. Many hotels, country clubs, or other decorated spaces already have their own color palettes that you can incorporate. If your venue is undecorated, you can be entirely original and choose what you like!

The important thing to keep in mind is choosing colors that flatter you and your partner in addition to colors you like. The groom will typically wear a pocket square in your base color, so if he knows he doesn't look good in lemon yellow, nix this from your list of options. You want to make sure everyone is looking their absolute best!

Design a Wedding Website

With the advent of the internet, wedding websites have taken off in popularity over the past few years. Wedding websites are a great way to display information that didn't make it to the invitations, advertise your registry, and hype up your big day in general! These are a great resource for guests who need to plan their schedules and want to know when and where to celebrate. Follow the tips below to create a streamlined website showcasing your wedding.

First, you should stick with the theme and colors you decided on at the beginning of this chapter. If you're throwing an elegant barnyard wedding, the website should clearly reflect that with its color, fonts, and images.

On the "front" page (the first page that shows up when you go to the link) provide all of the basic wedding details. This should include the date of the wedding, the address of the venue for both the ceremony and reception, and, optionally, who is included in the wedding party.

Tip*:*

If you post personal or sensitive information on your website (your mailing address for non-registry gifts, for example), you may want to consider using a password. This way, only the guests you know and trust have access to your wedding details.

On a separate page, offer more details about guest accommodations including recommended hotels, inns, or bed and breakfasts. You should include how close each accommodation is to the venue. On this page, you should also include travel details. Let your guests know where the closest airport is, and whether or not you will be providing transportation to and from hotels. <u>If you plan on encouraging your guests to use rideshare services such as Lyft or Uber, make sure they are available in your area first.</u>

Many couples choose to dedicate a page to local attractions or fun things to do in the area. If you have guests traveling from far away, they may choose to stay a few extra days and will probably appreciate suggestions on what to do. Name a few nearby towns and highlight your favorite cafes, restaurants, breweries, and any other entertaining places you can think of.

One of the website pages should be dedicated to your registry. Leave registry information off of your invitations, and link to the website instead. Your website is the perfect place for registry details, and it makes it easy for guests to simply click through and purchase something.

Since the wedding website is a reflection of you and your partner, you may want to have a page detailing how the two of you met. While this section is optional, it offers a fun peek into your love story. Most guests will want the long-story-short version, so just add the highlights leading up to your engagement rather than a novel. If the wedding location has a special meaning to you as a couple, feel free to include that information here as well.

Once you've completed your wedding website, don't forget to update it if anything changes. Remember, the website will be an information hub for your guests, and you want the details to be accurate at all times!

Book Your Entertainment

About 10 months before the wedding, you should plan on booking your entertainment. A wedding band or DJ is crucial to creating a fun and lively atmosphere at the reception. There are a few things to consider when making your entertainment decision.

First, consult your budget. While hiring a wedding band or DJ is generally traditional, it is possible to rock your reception without one if you're trying to keep entertainment costs low. Some couples choose to create their own perfect playlist and use a music streaming app and speakers (you can rent speakers for under $100). If you go this route, pick songs that will appeal to several different generations. Ask a close friend or a family member who is familiar with popular apps such as Spotify to be the honorary DJ and keep the tunes rolling throughout the night. Just make sure whatever app you use does not have advertisements!

If you want to keep things more formal, you'll have to decide between a band or a DJ.

The average cost of a wedding band is around $4,000; the average cost of a DJ is around$1,000.

The prices vary depending on a number of band members and equipment costs. You'll want to consider more than just cost, though. Think about the vibe you want at your reception and what your venue space can accommodate. If you have a large venue and want your entertainment to engage the crowd, a large band might be the best option. If you're limited by space and want a variety of songs played at the reception, go with a DJ.

No matter who you choose, try to see them live before committing. A live performance will give you a better idea of their stage presence, attire, and overall attitude. Most bands and DJs will have taped performances that you can consult. If you go with a band, make sure they know how to play the song you choose for your first dance. Same with a DJ— make sure they have that particular song in their library. Before finalizing your decision, be clear about songs you like and dislike. If there are any songs you specifically do *not* want to be played, make it known in your contract.

Music & DJ Services Template

General Information

Bride's Name:_____

Groom's Name:_____

Phone :_____

Email:_____

Wedding Date:_____

Reception Times:_____

Reception Venue:_____

Number of Guests:_____

Room Name:_____

Contact Person :_____

Guest Arrival :_____

Bridal Party Arrival: _____

Photographer:_____

Videographer:_____

DJ attire :_____

Indoor / Outdoor:_____

Elevator presence Y/N :_____

Reception Information

Cocktail Music (Y/N): _____

Cocktail Music Type : _____

Dinner Music (Y/N): _____

Dinner Music Type : _____

Introduction (Y/N): _____

Introduction Music Type: _____

Toast (Y/N): _____

Toast by : _____

Blessing (Y/N): _____

Blessing by : _____

Dinner Served (Y/N): _____

Style (Buffet, Family, Other) : _____

Cake Cutting (Y/N): _____

When (Before Dinner, After Dinner) : _____

Bride and Groom Dance(Y/N): _____

Bride and Groom Song : _____

Bride and Father Dance (Y/N): _____

Bride and Father Song : _____

Groom and Mother Dance (Y/N): _____

Groom and Mother Song : _____

Bridal Party Dance (Y/N): _____

Bride Party Song : _____

Bouquet Toss (Y/N): _____

Bouquet Song : _____:_____

Garter Removal (Y/N): _____

Garter Removal Song : _____

Garter Toss (Y/N): _____

Garter Toss Song : _____

Last Dance of Evening (Y/N): _____

Last Dance Song : _____

Other Special Dances (Y/N): _____

List Special Dances : _____

Allow the DJ to take requests (Y/N): _____

Discuss Catering Options

One aspect of the reception that your guests have to look forward to is the menu. There are several different ways you can approach the wedding dinner, and they will depend on your budget, the venue, and the number of guests attending.

First, determine whether or not your venue is providing a catering package (this should have been discussed during your initial site visits).

If your venue does not offer a caterer, ask for recommendations on who has been used in the past. This will give you a good place to start.

The typical catering package usually includes the food, beverages, staffing, dining rentals (plates, glassware, utensils, etc.), and additional fees (corkage fee, cake cutting fee, etc.).

There are many different serving style options to consider when planning the meal. Here are four of the most common types:

- **Buffet:** A more casual serving style where guests serve themselves at buffet stations. Nearly half of all couples choose this option.

- **Plated meal:** A formal, sit-down meal where guests are served their meal by a staff member. There are usually several entrée options that guests choose from in advance (usually by indicating on their RSVP) or on the day of the event.

- **Family-style:** Large platters are provided at each table, and guests share amongst themselves.

- **Cocktail-style:** Serving stations are situated around the venue, and hors-d'oeuvres may also be served. This allows guests to walk around and mingle while eating.

In general, a buffet-style meal is cheaper than a plated meal. While you will end up paying more for food, you do not have the added cost of servers. ***Buffets cost about $25-$30 per guest and plated meals about $40-$45 per guest.***

Once you settle on a serving style, it's time for the fun part: picking a menu! If you choose to have a sit-down dinner, your menu options will be more limited. The caterer will provide you with a list that you can choose from; luckily, the courses will complement each other, so you don't have to think too much about your decision. You *will* have to let your caterer know about any dietary restrictions your guests may have so that they can accommodate everyone.

If you go with a buffet, you'll have more flexibility. Variety is the key. Include several different "main dishes" such as fish, beef, chicken, and vegetarian options. Or, you may choose to go with a culturally significant spread. The important thing for a buffet is to have enough choices that even the pickiest eater will be satisfied.

At this time, you should also decide the type of bar (if any) you'd like to have at your wedding. You have a few options: a full open bar, limited open bar, and a cash bar.

A full open bar, which offers wine, beer, and mixed drink free of charge to guests, will run anywhere from $15-$90 a person.

If you're on a tighter budget, you may consider a limited open bar instead, which usually just serves wine and beer. The cheapest option is a cash bar, where guests pay for their own drinks. If you don't expect your guests to be drinking a lot, a cash bar is a way to go.

Catering Summary

Wedding luncheon / dinner	
Style (buffet / full service)	
Appetizers/hors d'ouvres	
Other dishes	
Multiple Meal Options ?	
1	
2	
3	
Number of Guests Served	
Costs:	
Food	
Setup / Service	
Other Charges	
TOT	

NOTES

_____

_____

_____

_____

_____

_____

_____

Have an Engagement Photoshoot

Taking engagement photos is a great opportunity to work with your photographer before the wedding takes place. Most photographers include an engagement session in their package as well. You may want engagement pictures to display on your website or use on your invitations. Not only are engagement photos great for you, but it will also give your photographer a chance to determine your most flattering angles, figure out poses, and experiment with lighting.

Discuss with your partner the type of photo shoot you'd like to have—candid or posed? Outdoors or indoors? Your photographer may have suggestions as well, so feel free to collaborate. Next, choose outfits that work for both of you. There's no need to match, and you should wear something that reflects your personality and style. Keep the accessories to a minimum to avoid distractions that take away from the overall photo.

Most importantly, have fun! Hold hands, kiss each other, and be affectionate with one another while the photographer works their magic. An engagement shoot is meant to put your love on display.

Check list

There are 10 months until your wedding! Have you...

Actions 10 months	Done Y/N
Chosen your wedding theme and colors	
Designed a wedding website	
Booked entertainment	
Discussed catering options	
Had an engagement photo shoot	

If not, consider completing these important steps before moving on to the next chapter.

NOTES

_____

_____

_____

_____

_____

_____

_____

9 Months Before the Wedding

You have made major progress with your wedding preparation. Keep the momentum up! Here are five more steps you should take nine months before you walk down the aisle.

Hire a Wedding Officiant

By now you should know whether your wedding is going to be religious or civil. If you are going the religious route and marrying in a church, your search for an officiant stops there—the pastor or other religious clergymen will perform the ceremony. If you don't belong to a church but would like to get married in one, you may be required to attend marriage counseling. If you are in a same-sex relationship and would like to have a religious wedding, it may be more difficult—but not impossible—to find an officiant. The United Church of Christ, Presbyterian Church, Unitarian Church, Episcopal Church, and Conservative or Jewish Reform Movement have been known to perform gay unions. For civil ceremonies, use websites such as <u>Thumbtack.com</u> or <u>GigMasters</u> to search for a certified officiant. Better yet, ask around and see if any of your friends are ordained!

Once you've settled on an officiant, plan to meet with them to discuss the ceremony. Ask how they plan to structure the ceremony and how much input you'll have. Most officiants will also ask you to choose custom scripture, poems, or other readings to be incorporated into the ceremony.

Shop for Bridesmaids' Dresses

Now that the bride's dress has been purchased, it is time to shop for another important piece of attire—the bridesmaids' dresses! While this may seem like an impossible task, since you will be dealing with different personalities, tastes, and budgets, there are many ways you can make the process less stressful.

First, be upfront with budgets. While this may be a sensitive subject, it will determine where you shop. Luckily, there are some options for bridesmaids' dresses no matter the price point. When discussing prices, don't forget to mention to your bridesmaids that they may need to budget an extra $25-$100 for alterations.

Initially, search online for inspiration. Pretty much every type of bridesmaid dress is sold by online retailers, and if you know where to start, it will save you time later on.

Tip: We suggest beginning the bridesmaid dress search as early as nine months before the wedding because you're more likely to hit a big sale this way!

Once you decide where you'd like to shop, schedule an appointment for the bride and bridesmaids to look at dresses. If you can't get together all at once, it's perfectly fine (and less stressful!) to schedule multiple appointments. You will want to make sure the bride's mother and maid of honor can attend as well. Initially, the bride and her mother may choose to pick a few favorites, then have the rest of the bridal party weigh in. This will help limit the number of options —and differing opinions—when you're just beginning the search.

Before your bridesmaids try on their dresses, it is a good idea to have them professionally measured by a seamstress. Every designer sizes differently, and you don't want a bridesmaid to have to make major changes to her dress down the road.

If the women in your bridal party have a variety of body types, you might want to consider choosing a color and fabric then letting the bridesmaid choose her own silhouette. This will prevent anyone bridesmaid from being forced to wear an unflattering dress. If you are set on all your bridesmaids wearing matching dresses, then have the bridesmaid with the most challenging body type be the first to try on the dress. She can then choose the dress that looks best on her and have the other bridesmaids follow suit.

The most important thing to remember when dress shopping is that you want your bridal party to feel comfortable, stylish, and confident. In the end, the dress choice is up to you, but you'll definitely want you and your squad to be on the same page.

Find the Right Florist

Flowers are a huge part of any wedding. As with your colors, they tie the aesthetic together and create the vibe you want to achieve. Different florists specialize in different types of bouquets and centerpieces, so look around and familiarize yourself with the types of arrangements you can choose from. Before visiting a florist, you'll also want to learn the lingo (especially if you've never heard of words like 'Biedermeier', 'nosegay', or 'pomander'!).

Next, assess your floral needs. If you want your ceremony aisle decorated in addition to arrangements, you may want to hire a florist designer as opposed to a typical florist. A florist designer will help you decorate the entire venue. Once you've assessed your needs, begin researching florists/designers in your area. If you're unsure where to start, browse local wedding magazines or ask for recommendations from family, friends, or the venue.

Once you have a shortlist of potential florists, schedule an interview. This is your chance to see their arrangements in person and have all your questions answered. The first thing you should ask is whether or not your wedding date is open, and if they have any other events that day. You may also ask how long they've been in the business and how many weddings they've done in the past. Finally, ask them if they're willing to work with your budget and let them know how much money you have to spend. Have the florist put together a proposal that outlines the total cost of materials, setup, and breakdown based on your budget. This will help you compare between potential picks.

Once you pick the right match, you can begin working on specifics. Provide the florist with plenty of pictures or inspiration boards, your color palette, a fabric swatch from a bridesmaid dress, and photos of your wedding gown. This will help the florist bring your vision to life.

While you'll want the final product to be as close to your inspiration as possible, be realistic with yourself. The flowers that most closely resemble your color palette might not be in season for your wedding, or the blooms you saw on social media may exceed your budget. In any case, your florist or florist designer will work with you to get as close to the desired product as possible. It's important to keep an open mind and remain flexible.

Book a Videographer

While photos capture snapshots of your wedding, videos can capture the real magic of the day—moments such as the exchanging of vows and toasts. Videography has come a long way from the bulky equipment and VHS tapes of ten years ago. If you choose to hire a videographer, here are some options as well as tips on how to make the most of your budget:

First, ask your photographer if they have any recommendations. Photographers often work closely with videographers, and some may even include videography in their package! If your photographer does not offer videography, The Wedding & Event Videographers Association (weva.com) is another great place to look. The most reliable and professional videographers will have samples on their websites for you to peruse. If they don't have samples or a website at all, this might be a sign to move on to someone else. Try to find videographers that match you and your photographer's style. If you plan on having sunny, well-lit photos taken, don't choose the videographer who only films in black-and-white.

The next step is to meet in person. Since this person will be following you around during your wedding and filming the most intimate parts, you need to make sure you get along on a personal level! Plan to meet with one or two. Once you've met, ask to see a full-length clip. While you may have already seen their highlights, a longer video will give you a feel for how your final product will turn out.

After the initial meetings, do your due diligence and find reviews for the videographers you're still considering. You may also ask the videographer for the contact information of couples they have filmed. If you speak to another couple ask them if they were able to capture the most important parts of their wedding and if they have a positive and professional presence throughout the day. And of course, ask if they're happy with their video.

The last step is finalizing a contract. Discuss with the videographer of your choice how many filmmakers will be present, the coverage time, what's included in the final product (a highlight reel, digital files, etc.), their cancellation policy, and of course, the total cost of their package. Remember, the photographer and videographer combined should account for about 18-20% of your total budget. Most videographers charge a flat rate based on the amount of time they will be filming. Make sure the price is in your range before finalizing anything.

Shop for Groom's Suit

Here are the tips every groom can follow when deciding on a suit:

Rent or Buy ?

- Renting will almost always be cheaper, so if your budget is on the smaller side, this may be the most sensible option.
  <u>The average suit rents for between $100 and $200</u>

- Buying a mid-range suit can cost between $300 and $800.

Some grooms may be put off by the idea of wearing pre-worn or pre-owned suits, but formalwear stores almost always have them professionally cleaned.

Once you've decided whether you're renting or buying, you can start researching which stores you'd like to shop at.

Tuxedos or Suits ?

- Tuxedos feature satin on either the pants or jacket and have a more classic, elegant look. If your wedding is black-tie themed, opt with a tuxedo.

- Both tuxedos and suits come in a variety of cuts and styles. Even if you decide to rent, you should visit a local formalwear store to be sized and see what suits look best on your body type.

Apparel Summary

Bride Apparel	Estimate	Actual Costs
Wedding Dress		
Shoes		
Undergaments		
Veil		
Jewelry		
Garter		
Hosiery		
Dress Bag		
Honeymoon Clothes		
Bridesmaid Dress		
Bridesmaid Shoes		
Bridesmaid Jewelry		
Bridesmaid Accessories		
Fitting Costs		
Alteration Costs		
Groom Apparel		
Tuxedo		
Shoes		
Groomsmen Tuxedos		
Groomsmen Shoes		
Fitting Costs		
Alteration Costs		
Rings		

Bride Ring		
Groom Ring		
Fitting Costs		
Engraving Costs		
TOT		

NOTES

_____

_____

_____

_____

_____

_____

_____

_____

_____

_____

_____

_____

_____

Ceremony Summary

Ceremony	Estimate	Actual Cost
Site Fee		
Security Fee		
Officiant Fee		
Marriage License Fee		
Ring Pillows		
Flower girl Flowers		
Site Flowers		
Bridesmaid Bouquets		
Bride Bouquet		
Corsages		
Boutonnieres		
Decorations		
Candles		
Musicians Fees		
Photography Fees		
Videography Fees		
Bride / Groom Limos		
Attendant Transportation		
Parking		
Wedding Coordinator		
Miscellaneous		
TOT		

NOTES

_____

_____

_____

Check list

There are 9 months until your wedding! Have you...

Actions 9 months	Done Y/N	Note
Hired a wedding officiant		
Shopped for bridesmaids' dresses		
Found a florist		
Booked a videographer		
Gone suit shopping		

If not, consider completing these important steps before moving on to the next chapter.

NOTES

_____

_____

_____

_____

_____

_____

_____

_____

8 Months Before the Wedding

While it still seems far off, your wedding will be here before you know it. Keep the ball rolling by accomplishing these three tasks eight months before your big day.

Rent Furniture

Your wedding reception is basically a large party, and parties need, well, *lots* of things. At this time, you need to plan to rent tables, tablecloths (often called drapes), chairs, plates (including dinner, salad, and cake plates), napkins, utensils, and glasses. Other common rental items include patio heaters (if having an outdoor wedding where it might get cold at night), lighting (string lights or others), cocktail tables, bread/food baskets, drink dispensers, and lounge furniture.

If you live in a large city or other metropolitan areas, rental companies are probably abundant. There can be key differences between them, and it's usually not their price, but quality. Wedding planners who regularly work with rental companies can tell you that some offer items of much lower quality than others: tablecloths that are too short or ill-fitting or stained linens, for example. If you are not working with a wedding planner, ask your caterer or the venue for a reliable rental company. Most companies also have a showroom that you can visit to gauge their quality and look at items in person.

Some other things to keep in mind when deciding between rental companies are their delivery windows, minimum order amount, and if dishware needs to be scraped clean/rinsed/washed. Certain rental companies also require you to open a professional account before ordering from them, so check on this requirement as well.

Next, you'll want to ballpark some numbers.
Here are the approximate costs of rentals:

- Plates – $0.55 each
- Forks/knives/spoons – $0.55 each
- Glasses (wine/beer/water) – $0.60 each
- 60" round tables – $9.50 each
- 60" round table drapes – $13 each
- 4' rectangular table – $6.00 each

- 4' rectangular table drapes – $.50 each
- Plastic folding chairs – $1.25 each
- Wooden folding chairs – $3.50 each
- Chiavari chairs – $9 each

You're not limited to renting. Can you buy all these things for about the same price? Sure! There are some logistics involved with buying, but if you don't want to deal with a rental company or a minimum order, buying is a good option. If you're having a more casual affair, checking out thrift shops and second-hand stores for dishware can save a lot of money.

Before buying, ask yourself if you have the space to store all of the items. If you have a tiny, third-floor apartment, buying might be out of the question. On the other hand, if you have a garage, basement, or spare bedroom that could deal with extra stuff for a bit, then great! Another thing to consider if you choose to buy dishware is washing and cleaning all of those plates, utensils, and glasses. When you rent, these items obviously come pre-cleaned, and most of the time, you can return them unwashed. If you buy, the dishware will have to be cleaned before *and* after the wedding—cleaning 100+ plates is no small task! If buying sounds like too much of a hassle, it's fine to stick with renting.

Here are some general notes on renting:

- If you don't know exactly how many guests you'll have, order on the higher end. Most companies will let you change your order close to the delivery date. It's much easier to drop a few tablecloths than to request several more for they might be completely out or your color might not be available anymore.

- If your venue comes without seating, you'll have to provide seating for both the ceremony and reception. If your ceremony and reception take place at the same venue, you'll only need one set of chairs. If your reception is being held elsewhere, you'll need to rent two sets. Plan to rent 5-10% more chairs than there are guests so that couples and families can sit close to one another.

- Also, order about ten extra sets of plates, forks, knives, and napkins. Some plates may be chipped, and if a guest drops a fork, you don't want to have them running back and forth to clean it.

- When it comes to glasses, you'll need to rent at least two for every guest. Guests regularly put glasses down or misplace them, requiring them to take another. Unless you can come up with a foolproof solution that makes guests stick to one glass, plan to have several extra available.

- Double-check that the delivery time and locations are correct before placing your order, and have someone else check, too!

Before finalizing your order, make sure you understand the company's policies and prices. Ask about delivery and setup fees, deposits, and their damage policy. Knowing these details will make the rental process easier!

Cake Tasting

What could be better than spending an afternoon indulging in desserts with the person you're going to marry? Nothing! That's why attending a cake tasting is such a fun and essential part of wedding planning. Here's the lowdown on what you need to know about it:

Start by thinking about cakes you have liked (or didn't like!) at other weddings. Keep a list going so you'll know what to discuss when you visit a bakery. Ask friends for bakery recommendations or read reviews online. Once you have a few options, make the call to schedule a consultation. Keep in mind that not all cake tastings are free, so get the details on prices during the call. In general, the fee is usually around $25—some bakeries may just add it to the total price of your cake.

When visiting a bakery, be upfront about your budget. This will help the baker choose the best cake for your price range (and if your venue is charging a cake-cutting fee, remember to include it in the cost!). If your budget is tighter than you'd like, you might want to consider a "fake cake." Yup, you heard right! A faux cake is essentially a Styrofoam base coated in fondant, and you serve your guests slices from a simple sheet cake instead. If you opt for fake but still want to have a cake-cutting ceremony, make the top tier of the cake real. Everyone wins!

Tip: Cakes are priced by slice, so consider asking the baker for around 20 fewer slices since not everyone will partake in eating the cake.

Before you attend the tasting, let the baker know which flavor and icing you like best. You have many options—from vanilla to red velvet, buttercream to fondant—so it's important to narrow them down. If you aren't sure of what you want, at least let the baker know what you absolutely do *not* want.

In addition to flavor, you should have a general idea of what you want your cake to look like. Keep in mind that if you want a cake with multiple trimmings, it's going to cost you more. Intricate adornments, such as a bloom of sugar flowers, are more expensive than small dots or pearls, for example. If you want flowers on your cake, consider using real ones! This could save you up to 40% on decorating costs. In any case, bring pictures of the type of look you're aiming for.

During the actual tasting, be sure to drink plenty of water in-between cakes to cleanse your palate. If possible, taste the elements of the cake (sponge, frosting, and decorations) separately. Then, taste them in different combinations to see which you like best.

Questions to your baker about cake choosing :

1) How long before the wedding will the cake be made?

_____

_____

_____

_____

_____

2) What ingredients are used? (Especially important if you, your partner, or the guests have any allergies!)

_____

_____

_____

_____

_____

_____

3) Which decorations cost extra, and how much do they cost?

_____

_____

_____

_____

_____

_____

4) How does cake shape affect the price?

_____

_____

_____

_____

_____

_____

5) How large is one slice?

_____

_____

_____

_____

_____

6) Will the cake be okay in warm weather?

_____

_____

_____

_____

_____

The Cake Summary

Flavor	
# of tiers	
Icing Color	
Accent Colors	
Toppers	
Miscellaneous décor/design	
# of Guests Served	
Slab Cake needed	
Costs:	
Wedding Cake	
Slab Cake	
Delivery Fee	
Other Charges	
TOT	

Note

_____

_____

_____

_____

_____

_____

_____

_____

Plan the Honeymoon

At this point in the planning process, it might seem impossible to focus on anything other than the wedding. But there's another major event you need to be thinking about—the honeymoon! Forget about the dress, cake, and flowers for the time being and focus on plane tickets and passports instead.

As with your wedding, the first thing you and your partner need to decide on is a budget. How much money will you have leftover to plan a honeymoon? More importantly, do you need to wait a bit before you can afford one? You shouldn't need to break the bank for a honeymoon. Some couples choose to wait to take their honeymoon, and that's completely ok.

Next, decide whether or not you'd like to use a travel agent. This is a busy time for planning, and a travel agent will do most of the legwork. A travel agent will cost you, but it could be worth the fee if you already feel in over your head.

Now, it's time to decide where you'll be honeymooning—easy right? You and your partner should already know your vacation preferences. Whether a white sand beach or the streets of Europe, you'll need to pick where you're going to spend your first few weeks as a married couple. Don't delay buying plane tickets. Booking early will help you find a non-stop flight. Nothing is more un-romantic than missing a connecting flight and having to spend the night in an airport!

Tip: If you have frequent flier miles waiting to be used, now would be a great time to cash them in.

Once you've bought the tickets, focus on accommodations. Decide if you'll be staying in a hotel or other nice place to stay that you can find in <u>Airbnb</u>. Look at and compare the prices between a few options. Next, you'll have to consider transportation. If you're staying in a major city, you can probably get by with using cabs or public transportation. However, if you're staying somewhere more remote, you'll want to rent a car. And even if your resort is all-inclusive, you'll still need transportation to and from the airport.

At this point, you should also purchase travel insurance, which will cost you about 5% of the total. Since your honeymoon will most likely be an expensive vacation, you don't want a hurricane or any other type of disaster canceling it. Travel insurance will also protect you in case you or your partner fall ill before leaving.

These are the major details of the honeymoon you should work out about eight months in advance. You can plan other specifics, such as activities and dinner reservations, further down the road.

The Honey Moon Summary

Wedding Night	
Hotel:	
Address	
Phone	
Fax	
Email	
Website	
Confirmation N.	
Price	
Destination	
Hotel:	
Address	
Phone	
Fax	
Email	
Website	
Confirmation N.	
Price	

Transportation	
Miscellaneous	

NOTES

_____

_____

_____

_____

_____

_____

_____

_____

_____

_____

Check list

There are 8 months until your wedding! Have you...

Action 8 months	*Done Y/N*
Rented furniture	
Attended a cake tasting	
Planned your honeymoon	

If not, consider completing these important steps before moving on to the next chapter.

NOTES

_____

_____

_____

_____

_____

_____

_____

_____

_____

_____

7 Months Before the Wedding

With your wedding seven months away, it's time to plan for pre-wedding logistics and finalize the details of your honeymoon. Once these steps are complete, you'll be well on your way to the big day as well as the dream vacation that comes after!

Book Transportation for the Wedding and Bridal Party

The perfect wedding starts with one major detail—getting there on time. Transportation mishaps can cause unneeded stress, so you want to make sure you hire vehicles well in advance. This is especially true if you are getting married during the spring/summer (April, May, or June) because it is also prom season, and limousine services will be in high demand. Don't feel obligated to go the traditional route, though. Antique cars, horse-drawn carriages, golf carts, or even something as silly as a tandem bicycle are all great forms of alternative transportation. It comes down to your wedding theme, what you feel comfortable arriving in, and, of course, your budget.

You can either choose to have your wedding party accompany you in your limousine or another form of transportation, or arrange a separate vehicle for them. If your wedding party accompanies you on the way there, make sure they have a way of getting back since you and your partner will most likely be sneaking off to your own hotel.

Another transportation factor you should account for is your guests. If you are hosting a lot of out-of-towners, you may want to consider hiring a charter bus or shuttle van to drive guests back and forth from hotels. Charter buses can transport about 50 guests and shuttle vans about 15, so multiple trips will most likely be needed. While booking additional transportation adds an extra step, it will help guests avoid parking issues and navigating an unfamiliar area. It also does away with the need for a designated driver at the end of the night!

It is important to book your transportation in person. If you book online, there's a chance you'll be disappointed when you finally see the vehicle(s). Do your research and read reviews before visiting a rental company, and ask questions over the phone to get a feel for how they operate. When it comes time to make the final reservation, you'll be shown your vehicle or a similar one to make sure you're 100% happy with the arrangement.

Most rental companies charge by the hour, so you'll want to plan accordingly when budgeting for transportation. We recommend booking a company for the entire day (from ceremony pick-up to after the reception) to avoid issues on the day-of. If a tip is not included in the contract, make sure to budget for that as well. A $20 tip for each driver is considered appropriate.

Transportation Summary

Car Service	
Vehicle(s) rented	
Total Cost	

Transport To Ceremony	
Name	Pickup Location & Time

NOTES

Hire a Hair and Makeup Artist

If the thought of doing your own hair and makeup the day of your wedding makes you nervous, consider hiring a professional to create your picture-perfect look. Start by looking for inspiration in magazines and wedding albums. The easiest way to get your desired results is by having a reference photo. If you want to give your makeup artist creative license, at least know what shades you'd like them to use.

If you're getting married locally, ask friends and family for artist recommendations. Chances are, somebody you know can refer to a stylist who has great reviews. Once you have a person in mind, book a hair and makeup trial to see if they're a right fit. Send them your reference photos and ask if it's possible to create a look inspired by them. Plan to time your trial as close to when it will be on your actual wedding day. This will give you the chance to see how long the process takes so that you can adjust whether you need more or less time. If you get your hair done first, discuss with the makeup artist whether they will be coming to you or vice versa. Plan for the extra travel time if you are traveling to your makeup artist on the day of your wedding.

It can take anywhere from two to three hours to complete your hair and makeup, so put aside plenty of time for getting ready on the morning of your wedding. If your stylists are also working with your bridal party, account for this extra time as well. If possible, hire a separate stylist to work with your bridesmaids.

Create a Gift Registry

Creating a gift registry is a wedding activity that both partners can look forward to. Ideally, your registry will be linked to on your wedding website and listed on invitations, so it's important to tackle this task early, as well before planning the bridal shower.

When registering items, only register those that you'll use and love. Avoid impulse decisions just because they caught your eye. If you already have a functional wine glass set, there's no need to register another. However, you may want to upgrade the chipped dishware set you've had since college. Do think about products you'll want to style your new home or apartment with. Discuss with your partner what your particular tastes and styles are, and see which items you agree upon. Consider what you'll need to host future dinner parties, casual gatherings, or a happy hour. Cover everything from simple serving platters to fine china. Since you'll want to cover a range of prices for every guest's budget, having a variety of price points is the way to go.

146

Tip: Some retailers might offer you a discount if you purchase the rest of the items that are left on your registry after the wedding is over. Ask around and see if this is an option before choosing stores to register at.

Feel free to register with more than one retailer. Having two to four registries provides guests with more options and is still completely manageable. If you choose to go this route, break things up into categories so you don't accidentally register the same item at more than one place (i.e., have one registry for kitchenware, one for décor, etc.). Feel free to register more items than you have guests, too. Your guests will appreciate having multiple options to choose from.

Don't feel limited to kitchenware and cooking gadgets. Décor is an important piece of your wedding registry. Throw pillows, blankets, and even decorative furniture are all appropriate to list. Or perhaps you're more into camping than cooking. In this case, a tent may be a better option than a fine china set. The important thing is, don't feel obligated to register only certain items. Choose gifts that fit your lifestyle and that you'll look forward to receiving!

Purchase Wedding Rings

By now, Do you want a simple band or something more elegant with embellishments? Do you want the wedding band to be the same material as the engagement ring? Decide these things before you go shopping and it will make the process easier.

Plan a time to shop with your partner and begin looking around. This is the fun part! Try on rings of all different styles and don't be afraid to mix it up—there's no rule saying your engagement ring has to be made of the same material. Aim to pick a ring that fits your lifestyle. If you work with your hands, avoid rings with embellishments that can fall off or trap dirt. If you play a sport, choose a ring that is comfortable and has smooth edges. In most cases, you will be wearing this ring 24/7. You want to choose one that works for you.

While shopping around, remember to stick to your budget. The more embellishments your wedding bands have, the more expensive they will be. If you choose to have your rings engraved, they will be priced by the letter and font used. If you want a personalized ring, but don't have room in your budget for it at this time, don't fret! You can always add or make changes to your ring later.

Before making your final decision, check to see if you can find the same ring for a cheaper price online. The same ring that sells for $1,000 at the store may go for $850 online.

Ring Budget

Ring	Price $	Fitting $	Size	Material	Style
Bride				White Gold	Plain
				Yellow Gold	Ornate
				Silver	Custom Made
				Platinum	Ready Made
				Zirconium	Identical
				Stainless Still	Different
				Wood	Embedded Gems
Bride Inscript					
Groom Inscript					
				White Gold	Plain
				Yellow Gold	Ornate
				Silver	Custom Made
				Platinum	Ready Made
				Zirconium	Identical
				Stainless Still	Different
				Wood	Embedded Gems
Total					

Make Sure Your Passports Are Up-To-Date and Take Time off from Work

Now that your honeymoon is booked, you'll want to make sure the following details are in order. If you are traveling out of the country for your honeymoon, make sure your passports don't expire before your trip. Although new passports can be issued in as little as two weeks, you don't want to wait until the month of your wedding to renew them. Take the time now to make sure your passports are in order, and save yourself a headache later on.

Next, prepare to ask your employer for time off. The typical honeymoon lasts for 10-14 days, and you don't want to wait until a week before to break the news to your boss. Giving plenty of advance notice is the courteous and professional thing to do. You definitely don't want work issues to ruin you and your partner's getaway!

Check list

There are 7 months until your wedding! Have you...

Action 7 months	Done Y/N
Booked transportation	
Hired a hair and makeup artist	
Created a gift registry	
Purchased wedding rings	
Made sure your passports are up-to-date/taken time off work for the honeymoon	

If not, consider completing these important steps before moving on to the next chapter.

NOTES

_____

_____

_____

_____

_____

_____

_____

6 Months Before the Wedding

Congratulations! You're halfway through the planning process. If you have completed all of the steps this far, you're on the right track. Keep up the great work.

Select and Purchase Invitations

Addressing invitations is a time-consuming process, so you want to begin the hunt for them early. Your invitations should hint at the formality of your wedding as well as complement the theme. Having your theme and colors nailed down will help you as you begin to look for **stationery**. If you have any wedding invitations on hand, use these as inspiration or browse stationers' websites for ideas.

Don't be afraid to get creative; while the classic choice for cardstock tends to be white, cream, or ivory with a black or gold font, feel free to play around with colors and fonts. Just make sure that the invitations are readable because that's the whole point of sending them in the first place! In general, avoid light fonts on white backgrounds and dark fonts on black backgrounds. In terms of font, make sure it's not too decorative. Overly scripted typefaces may be illegible.

When it comes to the shape and size, a 4.5" x 6.5" rectangular card is traditional. If you want to break from tradition and go with a non-standard card—think circular or scalloped—just know that it might increase the cost of your postage.

The following information should be included on your invitations: you and your partner's name, ceremony time and location, RSVP details, and the dress code (this is optional). Don't crowd the card with extraneous information—that's what your website is for. Lastly, do *not* include information about your registry on the invitation!

To determine how many invitations you'll need, start by counting households. Not every guest needs an invitation, and families only need one. The exception is for children who don't live at home anymore or people over the age of 18. It's also a good idea to purchase 10% (or around 25) more invitations than you think you'll need. This will save you down the road if you find yourself needing to send extra invites. Purchasing more invitations after your initial bunch is an expensive mistake!

Cost of the invitations:
- The average cost for most couples is between $300 and $650.

- The price hinges on many things: number of invitations, paper type, design elements, envelopes, and shipping. If you choose to add RSVP cards to the invitations, this may run you another $50 to $200.

To save money on invitations, consider the following:

1. *Skip engravements or embossing*
2. *Use standard, non-lined envelops*
3. *Send photo invitations*
4. *Send a postcard*
5. *Send an e-vite and have guests RSVP through e-mail*
6. *Create your own! (Keep in mind that while creating your own invitations can be a fun DIY, it is also time-consuming.)*

Hire a Day-Of Wedding Coordinator

If you haven't given much thought to hiring a day-of wedding coordinator, now's the time to do so. While they are called "day-of coordinators", this person will actually be helping you throughout the rest of the planning process.

The coordinator will begin by creating a comprehensive wedding timeline with you so that you are assured all the details will come together.

Day-of planning consists of the following:

- *Distributing the timeline to all vendors*
- *Coordinating the wedding professionals (hair and makeup artist, marriage officiant, etc.)*
- *Organizing the wedding rehearsal on the day before*
- *Helping the bride and bridal party with getting ready and taking photos*
- *Leading the bridal party through the processional and recessional*
- *Conducting a final headcount and counting place settings*
- *Placing favors and menus*
- *Double checking the floor plan and lighting*
- *Cueing the wedding professionals*
- *Collecting gifts and personal items*
- Helping guests depart
- Cleaning up and making sure vendors have been tipped

Your major consideration when choosing whether or not to hire a coordinator is the cost.

Wedding coordinators usually charge between $800 and $2,500 depending on the location, their experience, and the specifics of your wedding.

In general, the larger and more detailed your wedding is, the more a coordinator will charge.

It is up to you to decide if you'd like to pay for a day-of coordinator (but let's be honest—your peace of mind is priceless!). Consider the following scenarios that a coordinator is prepared to handle: wedding crashers show up and try to order drinks at the bar and need to be asked to leave, or the mother of the bride disappears just as you're ready to cut the cake. These day-of snafus won't fall on you to deal with if you decide to hire a coordinator.

Couples that choose not to hire a day-of coordinator may ask a close friend or family member to fill this role instead. While this is perfectly fine, you will want to make sure this person does not leave their post to get ready or partake in other wedding activities. It is also a good idea not to ask the mother of the bride to coordinate because there's a chance she will miss some of the biggest moments. Remember, your guests are there to enjoy your wedding too, so consider delegating day-of tasks between multiple guests if you aren't hiring a coordinator.

Organize Bachelor and Bachelorette Parties

The responsibility of organizing the bachelor and bachelorette parties falls to the best man and maid of honor, respectively. However, you need to discuss a few things with them before they can get the ball rolling. First, set clear expectations (and restrictions—did somebody say stripper?!). The bachelor and bachelorette parties are meant to honor the bride and groom, so you want to make sure your requests will be met.

Next, choose the date. One to two months before the wedding is usually a good time. It should not be too close to the big day, but not far enough away that the parties are anticlimactic.

Finally, discuss who is invited (obviously, the people you invite will also be invited to the wedding). Help the best man and maid of honor track down phone numbers, e-mail addresses, and any other information that's needed to get the invitation out.

And, that's it! The rest of the party planning (and associated cost) is entirely up to the best man and maid of honor. You can sit back, relax, and continue with the rest of your wedding.

Attend a Marriage Preparation Course

Even if you aren't getting married in a church or having a religious wedding, you may still want to consider attending a marriage preparation course. If you've never heard of such before, they are designed to help you and your partner build a stronger foundation for your future marriage. While these courses are often built on religious principles, you do not need to be religious to attend.

Most courses are broken up into five or so sessions that focus on the following values:

- *Communication* – for you and your partner to discover your communication styles and personality types
- *Commitment* – for you and your partner to learn about the benefits of being in a committed relationship
- *Conflict resolution* – for you and your partner to discuss potential relationship challenges and how to handle them
- *Keeping your love alive* – for you and your partner to learn how to maintain a healthy, loving relationship
- *Shared goals* – for you and your partner to find what is important to both of you as you develop as a couple

You and your partner will be coached through the course by a priest, pastor, or another married couple. What are the benefits of attending a marriage preparation course? For one, they help you and your partner start a dialogue about things you may have never given much thought to before. The course will also help you appreciate one another's differences, and realize you don't always have to be on the same page about everything.

While completely optional, a marriage preparation course will allow you to get closer to your partner and understand them on a deeper level. Wedding planning can be a busy and stressful time, so why not take some time to experience a bit of personal growth together?

Finalize Venue or Church Arrangements

Right around six months before your wedding, you should meet with your contact persons for the venue or church again to finalize some details. If you haven't done so already, establish setup and cleanup times. Figure out when the last call is and the latest that guests can stay. Ask about parking and where buses should drop guests off if you are providing transportation. Establish where the caterer is setting up, as well as the band/DJ. If you are getting married in a church, double-check the seating capacity. Working out these and other details far in advance will save you time later on.

Stationery Budget

Invitations Needs	Estimate	Actual Cost	Amount
Stationery			
Pens			
Reception Insert			
Reply Cards			
Envelopes			
Direction Inserts			
Transportation Inserts			
Accomodations Inserts			
The Event			
Wedding Programs			
Menu Cards			
Table Cards			
Place Cards			
Escort Cards			
Thank you Cards			
Card Types to be send			
Save the Date			
Bridal Shower			
Bachelor Party			

Bachelorette Party			
Rehearsal Party			
Wedding			
TOTAL			

Check list

There are 6 months until your wedding! Have you...

Action 6 months	*Done Y/N*
Purchased invitations	
Discussed bachelor and bachelorette parties	
Attended a marriage preparation course	
Finalized venue arrangements	

If not, consider completing these important steps before moving on to the next chapter.

NOTES

_____

_____

_____

_____

_____

_____

_____

_____

_____

5 Months Before the Wedding

The big day is getting closer—are you excited yet? We hope you are! Here are five more steps to complete five months before your wedding.

Book Rehearsal and Rehearsal Dinner Venues

The wedding rehearsal and dinner are fun and essential parts of the overall process—think of them as the party before the party! The rehearsal acts as a run-through of the ceremony so you can practice getting down the aisle and other ceremony specifics. Following the rehearsal is an even better event: the rehearsal dinner! The purpose of the dinner is to offer a more intimate space for the bride and groom's families to get to know one another, and for the couple to thank everyone that has been involved in planning the wedding. You may choose to invite just immediate family members or a larger selection from your total guest list. While the rehearsal and dinner usually take place one to two days for the wedding, it's important to book the venue or restaurant you will be using a few months in advance, so you're not scrambling for a location at the last minute.

Tip

Traditionally, the groom's parents are the ones who pay for the rehearsal dinner. Discuss this with both sets of parents around this time—they might want to host the dinner jointly instead!

Your rehearsal dinner doesn't have to match the theme of your wedding, either. If you're having a black-tie wedding, you might choose to host a laid-back backyard BBQ dinner. If you're having a casual wedding, consider having your rehearsal dinner at an upscale restaurant. Whatever you choose, try to host the dinner at a venue close to where you are actually getting married (and check with your venue beforehand—some include the rehearsal space in their package). If you are hosting out-of-town guests for both the dinner and wedding, they will appreciate shorter travel time.

When booking your rehearsal venues, have the following information on hand:

- You and your partner's name and contact information

- Name and contact information of the person paying the bill
- Details about specific rooms/spaces you plan on using
- A list of rentals (if any) that you will be using
- Number of guests who will be attending

You will also want to ask the venue if they have a liquor license and what their cancellation/refund policy is. While you and your partner will most likely not be footing the bill, also ask what the total cost and initial deposit amount is, so you can pass this information along to one or both sets of parents.

Buy Bridal Accessories

Now that your dress is purchased, you'll want to purchase the items that will complete your overall look. Bridal accessories that you will want to consider are shoes, jewelry, a headpiece (veil, flower crown, tiara, etc.), garter (if you plan on having a garter toss), cover-up (capelet, jacket, shawl, etc.), and shapewear (Spanx, body slimmer, bustier, slip, bra, thong, etc.).

Tip
Consult friends or family who were recently married and see if they have any accessories you can borrow. Many brides only wear their wedding jewelry or veil once, and you can save money by borrowing these items instead of purchasing them yourself.

The important thing when shopping for accessories is not to go overboard. If you're prone to piling on the flashy jewelry, you may want to consider scaling back for your wedding day. Less is more. You don't need a necklace, earrings, veil, tiara, *and* a sash. Your accessories should complement your dress, not distract from it. If your dress has a decorative or jeweled neckline, consider an elegant pair of earrings instead of a necklace. Own a simpler gown? Go with a statement necklace that will jazz up your look. If you're unsure about earrings, consult your hairstylist about what will look best with your wedding 'do.

When it comes to veils, you have many options. But the general rule of thumb is that your veil should match the exact shade of your dress. As with jewelry, you'll want to pick a veil that complements your dress. If your dress is flashy or has many details, opt for a simple veil. If you're going to show off the back of your dress (many modern dresses have sophisticated back embroidery), pick a sheer veil. The last thing you'll want to consider when choosing a veil is your body type. Veils differ in length and size and can accentuate different heights. If you are short or petite, consider going with a floor-length veil that will give you the illusion of height. If you're on the taller side, a mid-length veil will cut you in half and make you appear shorter.

More and more often, brides are choosing to forego a veil. This is completely fine! A well-arranged flower crown, decorative comb, or tiara can top off your look just as well.

If you are getting married during a cooler month or in a place of worship that requires you to cover your shoulders, a cover-up is a necessary accessory. You have many options for cover-ups, from cardigans to capelets to boleros. Again, if you are choosing to wear a cover-up, it should balance out the look of your dress. Use a beaded capelet to enhance a simple gown. If your dress is ornate, stick with a minimal accent such as a sheer cape.

Finally, you need to find the right pair of shoes. When shopping for shoes, don't skimp out on comfort. Though you want to look your best, you also want to *feel* your best. Nothing is more uncomfortable than walking down the aisle in a pair of shoes that are killing your feet! Choose a heel height that looks nice and keeps your foot stable. Also, look for shoes that are made from natural materials, as these tend to be more comfortable than synthetics.

In general, stick to your style when shopping for wedding accessories. The goal is to enhance your natural self, not make yourself something you're not.

Buy Groom Accessories

While the bride is busy picking out her veil, you'll want to shop for groom and groomsmen accessories. Just like the bride, you have many options, so don't wait until the last minute to begin looking at the accessories you want to complete your look!

The most obvious accessory is your neckwear. Bowtie or necktie? Silk or satin? Your neckwear should reflect the style of your wedding, from a black-tie affair to a casual beach affair. Your neckwear doesn't need to break the bank, either; you can rent ties for as little as $10.

The next accessory to think about is cufflinks. Cufflinks are a small part of your overall look, but consider matching the type you choose with the bride's jewelry. If she plans on rocking gold earrings, find gold cufflinks to match.

In addition to neckwear, a pocket square is an easy way to add color or a pattern to your look. If the wedding palette contains two contrasting colors, consider buying a pocket square in each and folding them together for a cohesive look. More neutral palette? Consider a pocket square with a quirky pattern to enhance your look. There are no set rules; the important thing is for the pocket square to be expertly folded on the big day.

When it comes to shoes, look for both comfort and style. Classic brown oxfords tend to look nice with navy suits, while black lace-ups complete a formal tuxedo look. If you already have a pair of shoes that you plan on wearing, have them professionally cleaned and waxed before the wedding.

While these are the main accessories you'll be shopping for, there is no shortage of other odds and ends you can add to your look: tie clips, leather belts, suspenders, lapel pins, and even funky socks! All that matters is that you look and feel your best.

Select Wedding Decorations

Now that the bride and groom's looks are complete, it's time to finish the look of the rest of the wedding! Decorations are a great way to showcase the wedding theme and your personal tastes. Choosing unified décor takes a good amount of planning which is why we suggest starting five months in advance of your wedding.

Since you already have a theme and color palette, you should have a good idea of what you want the finished venue to look like. If you haven't settled on a specific theme such as "rustic" or "fairytale" stick to a feeling you want to evoke instead—romantic, casual, or modern, for instance. This will leave room for creativity as you begin to stock up on items.

Begin with the essentials. You should already know what rental furniture you'll be using, so now it's time to think about centerpieces, table numbers, aisle markers, and the arch/altar backdrop. The typical centerpiece consists of a bouquet arranged in some type of vessel. If you haven't given your florist an accurate table number for floral centerpiece arrangements yet, now would be the time to do so. Depending on the type of flowers your florist uses, you may want to add accents to the centerpieces. These can include lush greenery, strands of pearls, feathers, or depending on the season, colorful foliage. You can find plenty of inspiration online and in magazines. Don't be afraid to think outside the box (we *all* know someone who has had mason jar-themed centerpieces). You may even choose to nix flowers from your centerpieces entirely—this is fine, too. Candles, potted plants, bowls of fruit, lanterns, and succulents are all great alternatives.

Table numbers and aisle markers should be simple and functional. Whether you choose to make your own or buy them, make sure you place them in spots where they can easily be seen.

You have countless options when it comes to designing the wedding arch and altar. Most arches have some sort of drapery, but it doesn't have to be fabric. If you are choosing to forego flowers in your centerpieces, consider a hanging flower wall on the arch instead. If you're getting married indoor, maybe a string light-themed arch is more your style. If you want to stick with simple, white gossamer curtains always add a classic look. Whatever you choose, remember that some of your best wedding photos will be beside the altar or beneath the arch, and you want it to look stunning!

Now that the "decorative essentials" are taken care of, take a hard look at your budget and see if you have room left for secondary details. These may include place cards or fun signage. If there is an empty space in the venue that needs to be filled and you have the money, consider splurging on a few items that can also serve your guests such as a dessert bar or a few pieces of antique furniture for people to lounge on.

Transforming your venue space is a fun part of planning the wedding, but not something you need to empty your pockets over. So, if you're the crafty type...

Create Your Own Wedding Decorations

If you plan on DIY-ing some or all of your decorations, now is the time to get started. The most important thing before you begin is not to go it alone – host a craft party or enlist the help of your family, but don't take it on all by yourself.

Here are some DIY decoration ideas that are totally chic and won't break the bank:

1. *Recycled bottles*: brown bottles with a single stem create a minimal yet rustic look.

2. *Spray-painted knick-knacks*: if you're incorporating a silver or gold theme into your wedding, consider spray-painting knick knacks to achieve a faux metallic look.

3. *Photo booth*: if you plan on having a photo booth available but don't want to dish out for an actual one, make your own! Balloons, hanging ribbon, or a flower wall make great backdrops.

4. *Natural features*: twigs, sprigs of greenery, pine cones, and wildflowers can enhance reception tables for absolutely free.

5. *Ribbon ties or streamers*: enhance any backdrop or even chairs with colorful bits of ribbon or streamers.

There are so many ways you can get creative—and save money—on wedding decorations. Take a trip to a craft store or look around your house for materials you already have before going all-out on high-end decorations.

Check list

There are 5 months until your wedding! Have you...

Action 5 months	Done Y/N
Booked rehearsal and rehearsal dinner venues	
Bought bride accessories	
Bought groom accessories	
Selected or created wedding decorations	

If not, consider completing these important steps before moving on to the next chapter.

NOTES

_____

_____

_____

_____

_____

4 Months Before the Wedding

With four months to go until your wedding, here are five more tasks to check off your list!

Book Your Wedding Night Hotel

If you aren't spending your wedding night at your venue, you'll have to book a hotel room. Booking four months in advance will help guarantee you get the type of room you want.

Most couples opt for a swanky suite where they'll get to enjoy all the amenities. When booking a suite, let the hotel know it's for your wedding night and ask if they have any sort of "romance package" you can add on. This usually includes champagne and flowers. Some hotels will even offer private airport transportation if you are leaving for your honeymoon the next day. Before splurging on a romance package for its convenience, see if you can find the same items à la carte for cheaper. There's nothing wrong with popping your own bottle of champagne!

If you're working with a tighter budget or don't see yourself getting into the hotel until late in the evening, consider choosing a mid-range room instead. Still, let the hotel know the room is for your wedding night for they might offer you a free upgrade!

Choose Ceremony and First Dance Song

For many brides, the wedding starts the moment she begins walking down the aisle—which means the right music is essential! The music sets the mood and enhances the emotions people will be feeling as the bride processes.

Decide on the mood you want to set. Traditional? Upbeat? Romantic? There's no right answer, and you don't need to stick to tradition. Organists or pianists have been staples of weddings for generations, but if you want live music, they aren't your only options. If you have room in your budget, harpists, violinists, or even a small choir add a great touch. There's nothing wrong with recorded music either. Here are a few song ideas to get your search started:

- *A Thousand Years* by The Piano Guys
- *Wedding March (from "A Midsummer Night's Dream")* by Mendelssohn
- *The Prayer* by Josh Groban
- *Clair de Lune* by Claude Debussy
- *Beautiful Day* by U2
- *Fairytale* by Enya
- *Canon in D* by Johann Pachelbel

As you can see, you have nearly countless options. Just make sure that whatever song you choose is appropriate. If you're having a religious ceremony, you'll want to run your song choice by the pastor or another clergyman who is officiating the marriage.

Tip: In general, you are not permitted to choose overtly religious music for a civil service.

Don't forget, you'll need a song to exit to as well! Your processional song should contrast your recessional song. If you choose a slower processional song, consider something more upbeat for the recessional to hint at the reception to follow. This song will be the first you and your partner hear as you walk out as newlyweds, so make sure it's one you both agree on.

Once you've decided on the ceremony music, you'll need to choose a song for your first dance. The first dance song is one you'll remember for the rest of your lives, and it should be one that makes you say "aww" every time you hear it after your wedding.

You and your partner will want to pick this song together, so start by thinking of genres you both agree on. Even if you like country and your partner prefers hip-hop, do your best to find common ground. If all else fails, you can always choose a timeless classic such as *Just the Way You Are* by Billy Joel or *Can't Help Falling in Love* by Elvis Presley.

When choosing a song, you'll want to be mindful of the beat and tempo. Upbeat songs may be fun to dance to later on, but for the first dance, you'll want something slower. If there's an upbeat song you absolutely want for your first dance, talk to the band or DJ—they might be able to slow it down for you.

No matter what, you want your first dance song to be sentimental and to reflect your relationship. Don't rush into a decision or wait until the last minute to decide on one.

Order Wedding Favors

If you would like to provide wedding favors to your guests, you should order them now. Wedding favors are optional, and many couples choose not to partake in them, but they are a nice way of showing your appreciation for your guests. Favors can be any small gift from personalized glassware (about $1.50 each) to paper coasters (about $0.20 each) to matchbooks (about $0.50 each).

If you are choosing to purchase wedding favors, order enough so that every guest gets one and a few extra for keepsakes.

Purchase Wedding Gifts

Wedding etiquette dictates that the bride and groom should purchase a gift for everyone who played a role in planning. This generally includes both sets of parents, the best man, maid of honor, groomsmen, and bridesmaids. If you have flower girls, junior bridesmaids, a planner/coordinator, or ring bearers in your wedding, they should receive a small gift as well. The gifts are usually presented at the rehearsal dinner.

Make a list of everyone who was instrumental in planning your wedding and start writing gift ideas next to their names when you think of them. A best man gift could be something as simple as a personalized pen or pocket watch—don't feel the need to go overboard.

The gift should show your thanks for his help in planning the bachelor party and giving a toast at dinner. For the maid of honor, classic gifts tend to include jewelry or a silver compact (you may even want to personalize this with her name). Whatever you choose, it should honor your friendship and all the hard work she put in organizing bridesmaids, going dress shopping, and planning your bachelorette party.

If you aren't as fond as physical gifts, or you know your best man and maid of honor aren't, consider experiential gifts instead. This could be a girls' trip to the spa or a guys' night attending a whiskey tasting. Tons of great ideas don't include items!

For the wedding party, matching gifts are totally appropriate if the thought of buying several individual gifts is too stressful. Something practical such as personalized beer mugs or colorful cookware are popular gifts.

Your parents (and grandparents!) deserve gifts as well. As with the maid of honor and best man, these gifts should be personal and a way of thanking them for all their support. Great gift ideas include a monogrammed robe or a gift card to their favorite restaurant.

It's hard to go wrong with gifts (the people in your wedding will appreciate the thought no matter what!), but if you're still unsure where or what to look for, online stores like Amazon or Etsy tend to have wedding gift categories you can use for inspiration.

Send Wedding Invitations (If You Did Not Send Save the Date Cards)

If you passed on sending Save the Date cards, now is the time to send your actual invitations. While it sounds as straightforward as mailing a typical letter, there are some important things to keep in mind before you begin the process. Follow these tips for nailing invitation etiquette:

1. Add a stamp and address all of the RSVP response cards. This is standard etiquette and will make it easier on the guests when they go to return them. While it would add a personal touch to address the response cards by hand, you can also use a customized stamp or stickers if you have a lengthy guest list.

2. Speaking of stamps, consider investing in some decorative ones. Post offices generally have a couple of different wedding stamps, but you can also find them online with sites like Shutterfly.

3. You might be surprised to know there is a proper order to assembling your invitations. First, the wedding invitation should be laid down with the words facing up. The response card is tucked face-up under the inner envelope flap (which should be stamped and addressed by this point). The invitation and any other cards (i.e., if you have a separate card for the reception) are then placed inside the inner envelope. The inner envelope is then placed inside the outer envelope with the front facing you. And that's it! Your invitations are now professionally assembled.

4. Weigh one of your assembled envelopes at the post office. If you used a uniquely shaped invitation or a heavier cardstock, you might exceed the weight for a single stamp ($0.49 for 1 ounce). Weigh one invitation first to avoid the surprise of having to double your mailing price.

5. Don't skip sending invitations to the obvious participants in your wedding—bridesmaids, best man, family members, etc.—*everyone* gets one.

You're now ready to send your invites off!

Tip: If you feel overwhelmed by the thought of addressing and sending all those invitations, ask your maid of honor for help. It is usually one of the duties she assists with.

Check list

There are 4 months until your wedding! Have you...

Action 4 moths	Done Y/N
Booked your wedding night hotel	
Chosen ceremony and first dance song	
Ordered wedding favors	
Purchased wedding gifts	
Sent invitations (if you did not send Save the Date cards)	

If not, consider completing these important steps before moving on to the next chapter.

NOTES

_____

_____

_____

_____

_____

_____

_____

_____

3 Months Before the Wedding

Acquire a Wedding Guestbook

Wedding guestbooks are a great way for you to remember everyone who attended your special day, and for guests to leave well-wishes for you as a couple (especially if you don't get to thank them personally at the wedding). The guestbook is typically laid out on a table for guests to sign as they begin to arrive. Since this book will be a keepsake long after the wedding is over, you'll want to purchase (or make!) one that you absolutely love.

Here are a few fun ideas you could incorporate into your guestbook:

- **Polaroid pictures:** Assign someone to stand at the guest table and take a picture of guests as they arrive, then tape the polaroid in the book. The guest can then write a personalized message next to their image.

- **Typed messages:** To add a vintage flair to your wedding, have a typewriter available so guests can type a message to you and your partner. Collect these messages, then bind them together into a non-traditional guestbook.

Guestbooks don't have to be an actual book, either. Consider an alternative that won't be relegated to a bookshelf once your wedding is over:

- **Postcards:** If you're having an outdoors or rustic-themed wedding, consider providing local postcards for guests to write their well-wishes on.

- **Corks in a heart-shaped frame:** If you and your partner have a love for wine, consider assembling corks into the shape of a heart, then having guests sign individual ones.

- **Personalized Jenga set:** Buy a Jenga set and have guests write messages on each block. This will make future game nights a sweet reminder of your special day.

There are endless ways you can get creative with your guestbook. Have fun with it—it's something you and your future spouse will be looking back on for years to come!

Create or Buy a Card Box

Along with your guestbook, you'll want to display a card box on the table that guests check in at. Card boxes can be anything from an elegant, wire-framed birdcage to a shoe box you jazzed up with ribbon or jewels. Just make sure the box is large enough to hold all the cards your guests will be bringing!

Select Ceremony Readings

Readings are a central part of the wedding ceremony, and you want to pick ones that are personal. Try to stay away from universal readings such as, "Love is patient, love is kind..." because those types of readings don't offer anything personal about you and your partner as a couple. Although these popular readings *are* beautiful, they have also been used in countless other weddings. Keep in mind that if you are being married in a religious setting, you may be limited to passages of scripture or other spiritual readings. Talk to your officiant about your options—even if the marriage is religious, you probably don't need to stick to the most popular readings.

If you are having a secular wedding, you can choose whatever you want. By selecting a more personal reading, it also gives you and your partner the opportunity to talk about what makes your relationship special. Start by thinking of pieces of writing you already know and love. Is there a poem that makes you emotional every time you read it or a song lyric that makes you cry? These are good places to start. If you and your partner are more private and want to stick to readings that highlight the general themes of love, that's fine too. The important thing is your readings are the right fit for you.

Most ceremonies tend to have two to three readings, and each should last for approximately one to three minutes. At this time, you should also be thinking about who you want to read them. Just like your readings should fit you and your partner, they should also fit the people you pick to read them. For example, you'll want to give a humorous piece to the comedian in your friend group and the love poem to a more serious friend. Once you have the readings picked out, give a copy to each person who will be delivering it. Although they will be reading from a piece of paper or a book, you want to make sure they're familiar with it—not looking at it for the first time five minutes before the ceremony begins.

Some couples choose to have their friends select their own readings to surprise them with during the ceremony. That's fine too! If this is the case for you, you should still provide a guideline on length. You also want to make sure the person knows you and your partner *really* well, and that they'll pick a reading that reflects you and your partner's values.

Choosing your readings can be the perfect break from the hectic planning process. Discuss your options over a romantic candlelit dinner, or read love poetry to each other while snuggled up in bed with ice cream. Whatever you choose, do it in a stress-free environment and make it romantic.

Attend Your First Dress Fitting

With three months left until your wedding, now is a good time to attend your first dress fitting. This gives you the chance to discuss with a seamstress any work that needs to be done. During the first fitting, you should bring your undergarments, shoes, and anything else that might affect the fit of your dress. Wear everything you will during the wedding (but don't worry too much about jewelry, unless you want to see the total ensemble).

During the fitting, don't be afraid to speak up if there's anything you aren't completely happy or comfortable with. The whole point is to communicate with the expert what you want to be done to make sure you look your best.

Once you're in your dress, move around! Take a lap around the store or even dance a bit to see how everything fits and feels.

If you need an alteration, decide that now and ask for a quote. Regardless of whether or not you will be having alterations done, you will need to schedule another fitting in about a month.

Tip:

To save money on dress alterations, opt for a local, independent seamstress instead of the services offered by the bridal salon where you originally bought your dress.

Around this time, you should also check in with your bridesmaids to make sure they have all received their dresses and that they fit properly. If any of your bridesmaids need an alteration on their dress, encourage them to have it done soon.

Send Invitations (If You Sent Save the Date Cards)

If you previously sent Save the Date cards, you can wait until about ten to twelve weeks before your wedding to send the invitations. Follow the same steps in Chapter 9 before mailing them.

Check list

There are 3 months until your wedding! Have you...

Action 3 moths	Done Y/N
Acquired a guestbook	
Selected ceremony readings	
Attended your first dress fitting	
Sent invitations (if you sent Save the Date cards)	

If not, consider completing these important steps before moving on to the next chapter.

NOTES

_____

_____

_____

_____

_____

_____

_____

_____

_____

2 Months Before the Wedding

Can you see the light at the end of the tunnel? Keep up your momentum as you reach the finish line.

Apply for a Marriage License

To make your marriage official, you'll need a very important piece of documentation—the marriage license! The marriage license legally binds you together as a couple, and it is how you later obtain your marriage certificate (which the bride will need if she's changing her last name).

Follow these steps to acquire your marriage license:

1. Apply for a license in the state and county you are getting married. Some marriage licenses expire within 90 days, so you don't want to apply for one too early. On the other hand, don't wait until the last moment to apply. Some counties have a waiting period of up to 72 hours before the license is valid. In other words, around two months before your wedding takes place is a good time to file.

2. Visit your county clerk's office. Both you and your partner must be present when filling out an application. Here is the information you'll need to complete the application:

   - Proof of identity: either a driver's license or passport. Some county clerks require a birth certificate; if you're unsure whether you'll need one, call in advance.

   - A witness: some places also require a witness to be present. Be prepared to ask a friend that you have known for a while to come along.

   - Parents' birthdays: you will have to provide information on your parents' dates of birth, birth states, and date of passing (if applicable).

3. Pay the license fee. The license fee is typically between $35 and $150, and most county clerks will have information about this on their website.

Once you've proven your identity, filled out the required paperwork, and paid the fee, your license will be granted to you! Some county clerks will give you a copy that date, while others will mail it to you within a few days.

To complete the marriage license, you will need several signatures. Both you and your partner, your officiant, and two witnesses (who are over the age of 18) will need to sign the license before it is considered valid. Once you have all the signatures, it is your officiant's responsibility to return the license to the county clerk's office. Once they receive the signed license, a marriage certificate will be mailed to you (in some cases, you need to pick the certificate up in person).

Reach out to Guests Who Have Not RSVPed yet

Not receiving all the RSVP cards you sent out can cause a major headache. And because your next step is to create a seating plan, now is the time to politely reach out to any guests that have not yet RSVPed to see if they're attending your wedding.

First, understand that timing is key. If your "RSVP by" date was June 1st, don't start calling guests on June 2nd. Many people probably put their cards in the mail the day before or on the deadline, so you could still have several on their way. Allow four to five more days before you begin tracking down those who haven't answered yet.

When it comes to reaching out, a phone call is always better than a text message. Have your partner call his or her friends/family, and you call yours. Once you have the person on the line, say something along the lines of, "____ and I are really hoping you can make it to our wedding. Have you had the chance to look at your calendar yet?" Chances are the person just forgot the RSVP deadline and meant to respond days earlier!

If you're short on time and decide you need to send an e-mail instead of hold a phone call, send individualized e-mails rather than a large group message to everyone who hasn't RSVPed yet. This is more personal and less embarrassing for your guests.

Create a Seating Chart

Now that you've gotten an accurate headcount of who will be at your wedding, you can draw up a seating chart. Creating a seating chart isn't mandatory, but most choose to because it will make sure every table is filled to capacity. A seating chart is also extremely helpful to the wait-staff if you are hosting a sit-down dinner (some venues will even require one in advance).

When beginning your plan, first take into account the shape of your tables and how many guests can be seated at each. Next, decide the order of seating at the head table. The head table consists of your wedding party and their dates if you have the room. If you are choosing to have a sweetheart table instead (just you and your new spouse), have your wedding party and their dates be the hosts of several different tables instead. Just make sure they have mutual friends at the tables if you go that route.

Typically, both you and your partner's parents will sit together at a table. This is also where your grandparents and other family members who aren't part of the wedding party will sit. This gives both sets of parents the chance to get to know each other better. If your parents are divorced, be considerate of where you seat them. If they don't get along well, consider putting them at separate but close tables. Or, if you have long rectangular tables, place them at opposite ends.

For the rest of your guests, you can categorize them by groups. Think of your high school friends, work friends, family, etc. You don't necessarily need to sit them all together, but this will help you see who knows each other. Try having a mix of familiar and unfamiliar faces at each table. And, of course, keep in mind those guests that might not get along— you'll want to avoid seating them at the same table.

If you know a lot of children are attending the reception, make a kid's table. You should also provide fun activities like coloring books or games to keep them occupied (chances are they won't find the reception as entertaining as the adults!). If there will only be one or two children, seat them with their parents instead.

If assigned *seating* isn't your thing, consider assigning general tables instead. This is a more laid-back approach to the typical seating plan, but it will also make it, so guests aren't scrambling for their seats as you enter the room.

By now you probably want to visualize the floor plan. Websites such as <u>AllSeated</u> and <u>WeddingMapper</u> allow you to create digital seating charts by dragging and dropping tables. You can also add extras such as the bar and dance floor to see what the entire layout looks like.

Whether you're creating or buying place/table cards, you want them to be legible. If you are not using place cards, an illustrated seating chart works just as well. The ultimate goal is to help guests find their seats quickly and efficiently.

Attend a Second Dress Fitting

Schedule your second dress fitting with two months left until your wedding. You should wear all of the same undergarments and accessories you wore to the first fitting. This is the time to make sure any alterations you requested at the first fitting have been taken care of and that the dress fits snuggly and comfortably. If you have any remaining concerns, voice them now.

Enjoy Your Bachelor/Bachelorette Parties

The last thing to do two months before your wedding is to enjoy the bachelor and bachelorette parties the best man and maid of honor worked so hard to put together. Remember, what happens in Vegas stays in Vegas!

Check list

There are 2 months until your wedding! Have you...

Action 2 moths	*Done Y/N*	*Note*
Applied for your marriage license		
Reached out to guests that haven't RSVPed yet		
Created a seating chart		
Attended your second dress fitting		
Enjoyed your bachelor/bachelorette parties		

If not, consider completing these important steps before moving on to the next chapter.

NOTES

_____

_____

_____

_____

_____

_____

_____

The month of Your Wedding

You've finally made it—your big day is just weeks away! The month of your wedding is undoubtedly the busiest. There are many small details you need to attend to, but don't see this as a reason to get stressed out. Follow the steps below, and it will be smooth sailing until the moment you say, "I do".

30 Days Before

Write Your Wedding Vows

If you are choosing to use your own vows (which you should!), now is the time to write them. It might seem daunting, but personalized wedding vows add a romantic touch to any ceremony.

First, agree on a tone with your partner. Although you may choose to keep your vows a secret until your wedding day, you don't want to arrive at the altar only to find you went the humorous route while your partner went sincere. Decide the tone together, even if you write the vows separately.

Think about all the things that make your relationship special. Keep notes on how you met and fell in love, and when you decided you wanted to spend the rest of your lives together. Think of the hard times you've endured and how you'll work through challenges together in the future. What do you respect most about your partner? What makes your relationship tick? Write all of these things down to get the process started.

Now that you have plenty of notes, begin by establishing the first draft. Wedding vows tend to follow this format: affirm your love, praise your partner, make promises, and finish with a final vow. While you can borrow inspiration from others, you want your vows to be unique to *your* relationship. For this reason, you should avoid clichés such as "love is blind".

Make your point without dragging on. Your vows should be short and sweet- around two minutes tops. Once you're done with the first draft, read it out loud and time yourself. If you need to, cut some words out and consider sending them in a letter to your partner instead.

Confirm Honeymoon Reservations

Around this time, you should double-check that all the details of your honeymoon are in order. Confirm hotel reservations, car rentals, and flight dates and times. If you haven't done so already, you may also want to make dinner reservations and plan day-to-day activities. You should also begin to think about what you will need to pack for your trip.

Pick up the Wedding Rings

If your wedding rings are being held at the store where you purchased them, schedule a time to pick them up. When you bring them home, make sure to keep them in a safe and secure spot. You don't want to be scrambling to find them on the morning of your wedding!

Delegate Jobs for the Wedding Day

If you didn't hire a wedding coordinator (or even if you did and you want to take a bit off their plate), now is the time to delegate tasks for the day of your wedding. You can even make a shareable spreadsheet with a list of tasks and let participants choose what they'd like to do. Someone might want to greet guests, while another person would feel more comfortable setting up centerpieces.

Confirm Numbers with Caterer

About 30 days before the wedding. you should give your caterer a final, accurate headcount. Also, make sure to provide them with a list of any food allergies your guests have.

Have the Groom Write His Speech

It is customary for the groom to write a speech thanking everyone involved in the wedding. This includes the bridesmaids and groomsmen as well as the parents. There are plenty of examples of groom speeches online that can inspire, and unlike the vows, there is no established format to follow. The important thing is to make it heartfelt and entertaining!

If the best man, the groom's father, or any groomsmen are making a speech as well, make sure they've at least started it by this time.

Break Your Wedding Shoes In

This may seem like an odd task, but for the sake of your feet, do it. Wear your wedding shoes around the house for a few hours at a time to make sure they're comfortable by the time you're walking down the aisle. If you find your shoes are still uncomfortable, buy moleskin, blister pads, gel insoles, or heel grips to wear on the day-of to ease the pain.

Check list

There are 30 days until your wedding! Have you…

Action 30 days before	*Done Y/N*	*Note*
Written your wedding vows		
Confirmed honeymoon reservations		
Picked up the wedding rings		
Delegated jobs for the day of		
Confirmed numbers for the caterer		
(For groom) written a speech		
Broken your wedding shoes in		

If not, consider completing these important steps before moving on to the next section.

14 Days Before Finalize Music

Whether you hired a band, a DJ, or you're just going with your own music, now is the time to finalize your choices if you haven't done so already. Send along the final list of songs to the appropriate person in case any last-minute changes need to be made. And if you are having a wedding band, make sure they know how to play your first dance song!

Have the Bride Cut and Color Her Hair (Optional)

If you decide to touch up your roots, redo highlights, or trim your hair for the wedding, do it about two weeks beforehand. You can also see if the hairdresser is available for a final practice run to get the look just right. Avoid making any major hair changes in case the result isn't what you were hoping for!

Have the Bride Acquire All the Paperwork Needed to Change Her Last Name

If the bride is going to take her husband's last name, she'll need to acquire the original marriage license. If one wasn't sent to you in the mail, call the county clerk's office where you filed for marriage and a get a copy. Hold onto it until after the honeymoon. The actual name-changing—obtaining a new social security card, license, and bank account—can wait until you get back.

Do a Final Walkthrough of the Venue

If your vendors are available, have them walk through the venue with you so they know exactly when and where to set up. If you hired a wedding coordinator, have them come along as well so that they know where to direct people.

Check list

There are 14 days until your wedding! Have you...

Action 14 days before	Done Y/N	Note
Finalized music		
(For bride) cut and colored your hair		
Received a copy of your marriage license		
Done a final walkthrough of the venue		

If not, consider completing these important steps before moving on to the next section.

NOTES

_____

_____

_____

_____

_____

_____

_____

_____

_____

_____

7 Days Before
Confirm Details with Participants and Vendors

About a week before your wedding, you will want
to confirm the details with all participants and vendors.

Begin with getting an estimate on how long the ceremony will last from the officiant. Take into account the readings, songs, and any other traditions that will take place. This information is important for your photographer and other vendors.

If you haven't already, provide a list of people you want to be photographed to your photographer. Create a timeline and communicate it with the people who are being photographed so they know where they'll have to be at specific times.

Ask your vendors how much you still owe them and when the final payments are due. Compare your numbers with theirs to make sure there are no accounting errors; if you find a discrepancy, make sure to speak up. You'll want to correct any mistakes before your wedding.

Get the contact information for a point person from each vendor, and pass the information along to your coordinator if you have one. It is important to get a phone number (and even a backup phone number!) because most vendors won't be checking their e-mail on the day of the wedding. Keep track of who is supposed to be where and when.

Finally, confirm with your venue what time you are allowed to begin setting up, and when everything needs to be taken down. This will help you establish a set-up/clean-up plan with each of the vendors. Ask the caterer how long it will take to serve dinner so that you can provide the band/DJ with a clearer timeline. If you are scheduling toasts before or after dinner, factor this information in as well.

Create a Day-Of Itinerary and Distribute

A week before your wedding is when you should write up a wedding day timeline or itinerary. The itinerary should act as a guideline, not the law—don't panic if the ceremony ends up running fifteen minutes over the time you wrote down! Most weddings end up running a bit behind or ahead of schedule. Perhaps you want to move the first dance up because dinner ended early, or you want to allot more time for photos.

Your guests will not notice a deviation from the schedule. The important thing is you start and end on time.

While you are the one creating the schedule, it should not be your responsibility to keep track of time on your actual wedding day. Leave that to your wedding coordinator or another responsible individual.

Here is an example of a typical itinerary for an afternoon wedding:

- 9:00 A.M. – Begin getting ready; bride have hair and makeup done
- 9:30 A.M. – Vendors arrive and begin setting up
- 10:30 A.M. – Photographer takes photos of bride/groom getting ready
- 11:00 A.M. – Photographer takes bride/groom portraits
- 11:45 A.M. – Photographer takes family and wedding party photos
- 12:30 P.M. – Venue doors open and guests begin entering ceremony space; pre-ceremony music starts
- 1:00 P.M. – Time listed on invitations (guests tend to show up a half hour earlier than this)
- 1:15 P.M. – Ceremony begins
- 1:45 P.M. – Ceremony ends
- 1:50 P.M. – Cocktail hour begins; additional family photos are taken
- 2:30 P.M. – Lunch begins
- 3:00 P.M. – Toasts are made
- 3:30 P.M. – First dance
- 5:00 P.M. – Cake-cutting ceremony/dessert served
- 6:15 P.M. – Couple departs
- 6:30 P.M. – Guests depart
- 6:30 P.M. – Cleanup begins
- 7:30 P.M. – All vendors leave the premises

Again, this is just a sample and you can adjust it based on the time of day your wedding is occurring. It should give you a better idea of how long each event should last though.

If your reception does not take place at the same venue where your ceremony was, you will need to include a gap in the schedule. If the two venues are within a half hour from each other, consider beginning the reception about two to three hours after the conclusion of the ceremony. This will give your guests the chance to grab a coffee, stop by their hotel room, or take a quick detour into town. A one-hour gap is *not* ideal because it doesn't leave much time to anything, and it is too long a time to sit around doing nothing.

Here is an example of a typical itinerary for an afternoon wedding with a gap between the ceremony and reception:

- 9:00 A.M. – Begin getting ready; bride have hair and makeup done
- 11:00 A.M. – 1:00 P.M. – Vendors arrive and set up for the ceremony
- 12:00 P.M. – Photographer takes wedding party and family photos
- 1:30 P.M. – Venue doors open and guests begin entering ceremony space; pre-ceremony music starts
- 2:00 P.M. – Time listed on ceremony invitation
- 2:15 P.M. – Ceremony begins
- 3:00 P.M. – Ceremony ends
- 3:00 P.M. – Vendors arrive and set up for reception
- 3:30 P.M. – Guests depart from the ceremony site
- 4:00 P.M. – Ceremony site is cleaned up and vendors depart
- 4:30 P.M. – Doors to reception venue open and guests begin to arrive
- 5:00 P.M. – Time listed on reception invitation; cocktail hour begins
- 6:30 P.M. – Guests move to dinner space
- 6:45 P.M. – Buffet opens/dinner is served
- 7:15 P.M. – Toasts are made

- 8:00 P.M. – First dance

- 8:05 P.M. – General dancing music begins

- 8:45 P.M. – Cake-cutting ceremony/dessert is served

- 9:45 P.M. – Last call for drinks/music starts to wind down

- 9:55 P.M. – Music stops

- 10:00 P.M. – Guests depart

- 11:00 P.M. – Cleanup is finished and all vendors depart reception space

Once you have written a timeline, distribute it to relevant participants. This includes the officiant, photographer, caterer, band/DJ, coordinator, wedding party, parents, and anyone else who is playing a role in your wedding. This will help keep you and everybody else on track!

Have the Groom Cut His Hair

Depending on how quickly your hair and facial hair grows back, go for a haircut/trim/shape-up around seven days in advance of the wedding. This could change depending on the type of look you want for the wedding. If you want a totally clean-shaven look, you might see if your barber can shave/trim your beard the morning of (having a professional barber do it will be much less nerve-wracking than if you had to!).

The important thing is not to drastically alter your hairstyle. If you have longer hair that you normally wear in a bun, now's not the time to cut it all off. Have your barber trim a few centimeters off and tidy up your edges instead of changing your whole look.

Attend Your Final Dress Fitting

Have the maid of honor come to your final dress fitting so she can learn about the details of your dress. If it needs to be bustled or if it has intricate straps, make sure she knows how to do those things—she's the one who will be helping you get ready after all!

You should also ask the seamstress how you remove wrinkles. Ask if you can use an iron, and on what setting. If not, ask if you should use a steamer instead.

Pack for Your Honeymoon

Instead of frantically packing for your honeymoon the night before you get married, plan to do it a week in advance. Here is our ultimate honeymoon packing checklist—all you need to do is tailor it to your destination and the season:

Tip: Don't pack anything you'll need to get to easily before your wedding!

The essentials:

- Airplane tickets (printed or available on your phone)

- Passport, visas, drivers' licenses

- Credit cards (only the ones you'll use)

- Any reservation confirmations (like hotels, restaurants, and events) not available electronically

- Copy of travel insurance

- Phone numbers of credit card companies (in case your cards are lost or stolen)

- Prescription medicine (in the original bottle)

- ID tags for luggage (inside and out)

- Camera

- Birth control/condoms/other contraceptives

For her (one week's worth of items – adjust for destination, season, and any activities you'll be doing):

- 1 pair of jeans, pants, or leggings (for cold airports and the plane)

- 4 casual shirts (t-shirts or tank tops)

- 1 light jacket or pullover (take one that is small enough to be stashed in a backpack/large purse)

- 1 nice sundress

- 1 cardigan (for chilly evenings/restaurants)

- 2 pairs of shorts (1 athletic/1 non-athletic)
- 2 swimsuits (bikini for the beach/1 one-piece)
- 1 swimsuit cover-up
- 1 pair of sneakers
- 1 pair of comfortable walking shoes or sandals
- 1 pair of evening shoes or sandals
- 1 purse or clutch
- Extra socks and underwear
- Bras (including strapless bras)
- Accessories (scarves, hats, jewelry, anything else needed to add variety)

For him (one week's worth of items – adjust for destination, season, and any activities you'll be doing):
- 1 pair of jeans or khakis
- 1 pair of nice slacks
- 4 casual shirts (t-shirts or tank tops)
- 2 polo or button-down short-sleeved shirts
- 1 light jacket or pullover (take one that is small enough to be stashed in a backpack)
- 2 pairs of shorts (1 athletic/1 non-athletic)
- 1 sports jacket (for nicer restaurants)
- 1 swimsuit
- 1 pair of sneakers
- 1 pair of comfortable walking shoes or sandals
- 1 pair lace-ups
- Extra socks and underwear

Toiletries:
- Travel-sized toothpaste
- Toothbrushes

- Deodorant
- Makeup
- Makeup remover
- Cotton balls and swabs
- Comb and/or brush
- Hair gel or spray
- Nail file/clippers
- Shaving cream
- Razors
- Contact lenses, case, eye drops
- Hairbrush
- Hair ties/headband/clips

Items to buy before arriving at destination:

- Sunscreen and lip balm
- Sunglasses
- Sun hat/baseball cap
- Insect repellent and itch cream
- Aloe vera
- Band-Aids
- Medicine (Aspirin, Antacid, Antihistamine, Motion Sickness, Diarrhea)
- Feminine hygiene products (these can be hard to come by depending on where you go)
- Paperback books
- Deck of cards
- Canvas bag for the beach or pool
- Guidebook

- Electrical converter/adapter

Miscellaneous:

- Extra pair of glasses and/or contacts
- Inhaler
- Ziplock bags of all sizes (they make handy waterproof bags)
- Earplugs
- Stain-removing pen
- Hand sanitizer
- Sewing kit
- Small backpack for day trips
- 1 pair of old sneakers you're willing to get dirty
- 1 pair workout of sneakers
- 2 to 3 workout outfits if you plan on working out
- Swiss Army knife
- Umbrella and other rain gear

Check list

There are 7 days until your wedding! Have you...

Action 7 days before	Done Y/N
Confirmed details with vendors and participants	
Created day-of itinerary	
(For groom) trimmed hair	
Attended your final dress fitting	
Packed for your honeymoon	

If not, consider completing these important steps before moving on to the next section.

NOTES

_____

_____

_____

_____

_____

_____

_____

2-3 Days Before

Attend Rehearsal and Rehearsal Dinner

Your rehearsal and rehearsal dinner should take place two to three days before your wedding. Don't stress over this part for they are meant to be a fun way to thank the VIPs of your wedding.

The dinner begins with a toast from the hosts (usually the groom's parents, unless the parents of both bride and groom helped organize the event), followed by a toast from the groom to the bride and her family.

If you want to cut down on the number of people speaking at your reception, you may want to schedule some of those toasts for this dinner. And if there's anyone who wants to poke a bit of fun at either the bride or the groom, this is the more appropriate setting.

After dinner and dessert, it's time to present your wedding gifts. Present your gifts to the wedding party/other wedding participants first, followed by the best man and maid of honor, and finally your parents/family.

Allow time for family and friends on both the bride and groom's side to mingle. Before everyone heads home for the night, briefly go over the wedding timeline and let everyone know if there have been any last-minute changes.

Pick up Dress

You should plan to pick up your wedding dress the day after the rehearsal. Check the dress over one last time to make sure there isn't any missing beading, lace, loose stitches, etc. Once you're satisfied the dress is in mint condition, you can leave. Make sure when transporting the dress that it is covered and protected from the elements.

Pick up Groom's and Groomsmen's Suits

You should also plan to pick up your suit the day after the rehearsal and have the groomsmen pick up their suits as well. Make sure when you pick up your suit that it is clean and wrinkle-free.

Have Bride Get Nails Done and Attend to Any Last-Minute Beauty Needs

If you plan on having your nails professionally done, do them two to three days before the wedding. You'll probably want to opt for a gel manicure because your paint job will have less of a chance of becoming chipped or cracked than a regular manicure. If you need your eyebrows, lips, underarms, or any other body part waxed now is the time to do so as well. Avoid waxing the day before the wedding as there's a chance you'll still have red skin.

Confirm Transportation Details With Rental Company

If you rented transportation, call the rental company to confirm pickup and drop-off times. Even though you'll want these times to be as accurate as possible, give yourself a 20-minute window time on the day of your wedding to account for traffic and other variables.

Check list

There are 2-3 days until your wedding! Have you...

Action 2-3 days before	*Done Y/N*
Attended the rehearsal and rehearsal dinner	
Picked up your dress	
Picked up your suit	

Had your nails done	
Confirmed transportation details	

If not, consider completing these important steps before moving on to the next section.

NOTES

_____

_____

_____

_____

_____

_____

_____

_____

_____

_____

_____

_____

The Day Before

There are only two things you should do the day before your wedding: relax and get a good night's sleep. You have a big day ahead of you, so keep the activity to a minimum!

The Wedding Day

The biggest thing to do the morning of your wedding is...breath. Then, congratulate yourself on how far you've come: you survived a whole year of planning!

There are just a few small items you need to take care of before walking down the aisle. First, make sure the wedding rings are given to the best man for safekeeping. Next, make sure the coordinator or designated family member has the remainder of the payment for all the vendors. Finally, make sure all the participants have their flowers and any other items that are needed for the ceremony. The coordinator and your wedding party can handle the rest of the logistics for the day.

Chances are if you followed the advice in this book, your wedding will go off without a hitch. But don't worry if small details don't go exactly as planned throughout the day. The most important thing to do on your wedding day is to relax and have fun. It may very well be the best day of your life!

Now, it's time to enjoy it.

Costs Summary

Category	Budget	Spent	Difference + / -
Ceremony			
Site Rental			
Officiant			
Rental Fees:			
Chairs			
Misc			
Reception			
Site Rental			
Other Rental Fees			
Decorations			
Food			
Cake			
Beverages			
Bar			
Bridal Gown			

Dress			
Veil/Headpiece			
Shoes			
Foundation Garments			
Jewelry			
Hair & Beauty			
Hair Salon			
Spa			
Makeup			
Man's Wear			
Tuxedo Rental			
Tuxedo Buying			
Groomsman Rental			
Groomsman Buying			

Music			
Wedding			
Reception:			
DJ			
Band			
Flowers			
Ceremony Site			
Reception			
Bouquets			
Corsages			
Stationery			
Invitations			

Photography			
Portratits / Candids			
Videography			
Miscellaneous			
Favors			
Transportation			

Conclusion

Thanks for making it through to the end of *The Wedding Planner and Organizer*. We hope that it was informative and able to provide you with all the tools you need to plan the perfect wedding. Since you've made it this far, chances are that you're well on your way. If you found this book helpful in any way, a review on Amazon would be greatly appreciated!

Even if your wedding is more than a year off, you can take the steps outlined at the beginning of this book—it never hurts to start planning early. Consider printing the worksheets, checklists, and other tables and storing them in your wedding binder for future use. The tasks were ordered in a way that gives you plenty of time to accomplish them. By sticking to the general twelve-month timeline, there's a better chance you will have everything done on time before the wedding.

And last but not least, enjoy your happily ever after!

60147374R00119

Made in the USA
Middletown, DE
13 August 2019